The Lawyer in Society

Leon Jaworski
Senior partner, Fulbright and Jaworski, Houston, Texas; LL.M.,
George Washington University, 1926; LL.B., Baylor University, 1925.

The Lawyer in Society

LEON JAWORSKI

Cover Design by David Alcorn

Library of Congress Cataloging-in-Publication Data

Jaworski, Leon.
 The lawyer in society / Leon Jaworski.
     p. cm.
  ISBN 978-1-60258-072-5 (pbk. : alk. paper)
 1. Lawyers--United States. 2. Practice of law--United States. I. Title.
  KF298.J39 2007
  340.023>73--dc22
                    2007028565

Printed in the United States of America on acid-free paper with a minimum of 30% pcw recycled content.

Foreword

In September of 1980 Leon Jaworski presented a series of lectures at Baylor Law School on the subject The Lawyer in Society. The lectures provided a valuable view of the legal profession and its impact on American society, through the eyes of a person who has contributed greatly to both. The following booklet is made up of Mr. Jaworski's prepared lectures and transcriptions of the tape-recorded question and answer sessions that followed them.

Mr. Jaworski is Past President of the American Bar Association, Past President of the State Bar of Texas, and Past President of the American College of Trial Lawyers. He served as Special Prosecutor of the Watergate Special Prosecution Force (1973-1974), and Special Counsel to the U.S. House of Representatives Committee on Standards of Official Conduct (1977-1978). In World War II, Mr. Jaworski served as a Colonel in the Judge Advocate General's Department. He served as Trial Judge Advocate in major World War II military trials held in the United States and later served as Chief of War Crimes Trials Section of the U.S. Army in the European Theatre.

Contents

The Lawyer in Society

I

The Lawyer's Role in Our Past

A good place to begin in this series of lectures is to take a panoramic look at the lawyers' historical status from biblical days forward. Whereas the lawyer of today draws a modicum of respect from his fellowman and is assigned a reasonably respectable place in our society, this has not always been the case.

Recently there came to my attention an article disparaging lawyers. It began with a quote from the New Testament which was not unfamiliar to me. It was taken from the eleventh chapter of Luke. The gospel writer Luke was quoting his version of the words of the Master to this effect: "And (Jesus) said 'Woe unto you lawyers also! for ye load men with burdens grievous to be borne, and ye yourselves touch not the burdens with one of your fingers!' "

Now I believe in Holy Writ. In fact, I swear by the Bible, although I cannot assert that I have always lived by its teachings. I often quote it—especially when it supports what I espouse. But this particular passage in the gospel according to Luke troubles me. I do not want to believe that my Master held such a low opinion of lawyers, and I sought a rationalization. I finally came to this conclusion. Luke, you will recall, was a physician and in those days a physician practiced all kinds of medicine, including surgery. I have concluded that at some point in his career, Dr. Luke must have been a defendant in a malpractice suit and thus formed a jaundiced view of lawyers. This same article to which I referred vaulted from the biblical days to modern times by saying: "Lawyers have since overburdened more than a few societies."

The facts are that the legal profession throughout English and American histories has had its peaks and its valleys in public appraisal. Because so much of our body of law stems from English law, it may be well to take a brief look first at the lawyer's stature in England as long as three centuries ago, in this country during the 17th Century, and in the

18th Century before the Revolution and finally, following the Revolution. To do so will also give us a better understanding of the evolution of law in our country.

At the end of the 17th Century in England, the lawyer sank to such a low place in public esteem that he was considered a parasite. Boswell, in his volume on the "Life of Dr. Johnson," referred to an individual who said that "he did not care to speak ill of any man behind his back, but he believed the gentleman was an attorney." So in Boswell's day, to call a man a lawyer was similar to calling him an S.O.B. nowadays. In fact, at one time in England there seemed to be an "open season" on lawyers. You will recall that Shakespeare in one of his plays observed: "first thing we do is kill all the lawyers."

It was not much better in our country in the first part of the 17th Century at the time of the establishment of settlements by American colonists. The situation was not precisely the same in each colony, for each had a somewhat different background, and for a number of years due to difficulty in travel and other reasons there was not much contact between these colonies.

You will recall that most of the colonists had left England because of conditions they considered oppressive, and they sought a new land where they would be free of such tyrannical conduct. They did not bring with them a feeling of respect for the law of England as it existed at that time. The same was true of their view of lawyers.

It has been noted in some books dealing with this early history that, in Pennsylvania for instance, the influence of the Quakers was such as to leave no place for the lawyer and that in New York the merchants were disposed to keep matters in their own hands. In some of the colonies, notably Massachusetts, laws were predicated primarily on the Bible. Resort was not had to lawyers to interpret these but rather to those who were theoretically versed in the art of divinity. The best histories available indicate that whereas some individuals had been committed to act as attorneys, as late as 1700 no one in Massachusetts had been trained for the practice of law. With the coming of the 18th Century, a few more lawyers were recorded to have been present. Their training or lack of training is not known.

A. *Historical Examples*

It is well for us to pause to take note of what conditions were like during the period of time just mentioned when there were no lawyers among the early colonies. Let's take Salem, Massachusetts as an example.

We are told that between June 10 and September 22, 1692, nineteen

Massachusetts men and women and two dogs were hanged for witchcraft, and one man was pressed to death for refusing to plead to the indictment. When the executions came to an end, fifty-five people had confessed that they were witches, and a hundred and fifty were in jail either waiting to be tried or enduring, as several convicted women did, reprieves granted them so that infants they had already conceived would not be executed with them.[1]

We are told that one set of trials on June 29, 1692 moved swiftly, for the trial proceedings consisted primarily of the reading of depositions that were taken earlier from so-called witnesses at "examinations" that were conducted by magistrates that had been appointed by the governor. The following excerpt gives a good account of how the trials proceeded and the disposition that was made:

> Five witches were hanged on July 19; five more on August 19; and eight on September 22. On September 19, Giles Cory, an old man who did not want his heirs to be deprived of his property by a bill of attainder, had to pay for his foresightedness; refusing to plead either guilty or not guilty, he avoided conviction but had to endure being pressed to death under increasing weights of stone as the sheriff, in accordance with British common law, tried to force him to answer the indictment.

The witchcraft delusion had brought all kinds of oppressions, injustices and wrongful executions. The process was steamrolling until suddenly it got so bad that the authorities became alarmed. There was a "crying out" against innocent people by those who wanted to hurt them, and more and more victims were brought to "trial" and sentenced. Then there came a sudden reversal of public opinion, and although witchcraft was still considered to be a real danger, the crime of spilling innocent blood appeared to the authorities to be more frightening than the crime of permitting a witch to live.

The so-called trials were abominations with "spectral evidence" serving as a basis for the convictions. The reason for this episode of blight and stain on the history of these colonies can be attributed primarily to the absence of lawyers. There was none who either prosecuted or defended. The entire proceeding was one without regard to rules of evidence and without regard to any rule of law.

Some of these witchcraft trials were held in an upstairs room in a building still standing in Salem, Massachusetts. I visited it a number of years ago. I stood there with a mixture of thoughts. Of course one of them related to the difference there would have been had there been lawyers to stand up for the rights of the individuals so unjustly accused.

[1] D. LEVIN, WHAT HAPPENED IN SALEM? (2d ed. 1960).

Another thought that swept my mind was the cowardice of the judges who permitted themselves to be used as tools. But there was another thought that visited me—one of somewhat recent vintage—and I wondered how far removed the witchcraft trials were from some of the conduct that I had witnessed during my lifetime.

When I was a student here at Baylor, in the early 20's in this very city, there was an episode not too far removed from the atrocities of Salem. Someone had cried out against a white man suspected of furthering prostitution—he was a "pimp," they charged. At high noon one bright day he was accosted by two carloads of Ku Klux Klansmen in their robes of white. He was kidnapped, whisked out to a remote spot in Cameron Park, his clothes were removed and his body tarred and feathered. The police, not knowing who was behind it all, came upon the scene and to their embarrassment found the Klansmen doing their dirty work— serving as accusers, indicters, judge, jury and executioners—all wrapped in one. Obviously, charges had to be filed, and they were charged with whitecapping, which involved the statutory offense of wearing a hood while engaged in the unlawful pursuit of terrorism. An examining trial was held, and I attended. Much to my surprise, a prominent banker in the building where I worked part-time as a legal secretary was among the defendants. Waco and McLennan County were then controlled by the Klan. The public officials who dealt with this matter were beholden to the Klan, and as a consequence the lawbreakers were never brought to trial. Here—in the workings of the Klan—you have a striking example of the breakdown of the rule of law. In its place, and as a substitute, there existed a rule of men and of force—a return to the law of the jungle.

I mention this incident especially because it illustrates what happens (a) to our rights and liberties when forces outside the rule of law take over and (b) when lawyers in a community do not stand up for law and order. In Waco, at that time, not only were members of the Bar failing in their duty, but public officials who were lawyers—judges, prosecutors, and others—had scorned their oaths of office by taking a conflicting oath of the Klan. One official—a district judge—a great American and a noble disciple of the rule of law, refused to take this oath. His name is James P. Alexander, then a teacher at Baylor Law School of the practice court course now taught by Professor Matt Dawson.

But let me return to the 17th Century. Although the early colonists did not have the benefit of legal representation by members of a trained profession, they did bring with them a history of law which it is appropriate for us to recognize at this point.

B. *The English Influence*

Last year I stood in the meadow at Runnymeade where King, prelates and nobles gathered in confrontation. For me, it was an occasion of reflection on the eventual impact of this historic event on the freedoms my fellow-Americans and I enjoy. Not long after, I revisited Independence Hall in Philadelphia where, after ten years of intense and sometimes highly divisive effort, our Constitution was adopted. This time my reflections took me back to Magna Carta. My thoughts were haunted by the question—hypothetical to be sure, but germane—without the Great Charter of England, would there have been a Constitution of the United States?

Historians and legal scholars make reference to several sources of our liberty. Not all name the same. But none fails to include Magna Carta. Indeed, most of them embrace the Great Charter as a *primary* source.

When John Adams, an able and courageous lawyer and patriot, was attacking the Stamp Act, he cited Magna Carta as supporting his argument on the injustice of "taxation without representation." This ignited in the Colonists a deep and widespread emotional fervor of resentment and resistance. To them it meant that King George was trampling on a sacred document, and they would have none of it. No greater rallying cry could have been sounded.

The Chief Justice of the United States Supreme Court recently told us that the fifteenth paragraph of the Great Charter, which promised that Englishmen who went forth to colonize new worlds would enjoy all the rights of Englishmen, became the juridical basis of our later Declaration of Independence. He points out that this dream of Magna Carta found expression as early as 1606 in the First Charter of Virginia and later in the Charter of New England in 1620.

An early opinion of our Supreme Court[2] written in 1819 is one of many in which references are made to Magna Carta. In the body of the Court's opinion, it is stated that "after volumes spoken and written (about the guarantees of Magna Carta)—the good sense of mankind has at length settled down to this: that they were intended to secure the individual from the arbitrary exercise of the powers of government."

Of the many written passages referring to the influence of Magna Carta on American liberties, I like best the words of Lord Denning, the Master of The Rolls, a universally admired English jurist I am privileged to call my friend. Speaking at Runnymeade a few years ago, he put it this way:

> Some bold and venturesome men sailed across the seas from this island. They founded the colonies of Virginia, Massachusetts, Pennsylvania and others. They took with them the 'rights of Englishmen.' When they decided in 1776 to make their Declaration of

[2]The Bank of Columbia v. Okley, 17 U.S.(4 Wheat.) 235, 244 (1819).

Independence, they said of George III what the Barons said of King John: 'The history of the present King of Great Britain is a history of repeated injuries and usurpation.'

When they came to draft the Constitution, they used in the Fifth Amendment words which came by direct succession from Magna Carta: 'No Person . . . shall be deprived of life, liberty or property, without due process of law.'

So they established the rule of law in the greatest country of the world, the United States of America. It was established as those here in 1215 determined it should be—established forever.

Legal scholars confirm what Lord Denning has told us. They assure us that no clause of Magna Carta has been cited more often as a guarantee of the liberties of the citizen than Chapter 39 which became Chapter 29 in the reissue of Henry III in 1225. This Chapter provides that no free man shall be imprisoned, dispossessed, banished or destroyed, "except by the legal judgment of his peers or by the law of the land." English law books of the twelfth century trace this phrase, "the law of the land, " to documents of the Holy Roman Empire in the 11th Century. It is quite reasonable to deduce, therefore, that "the law of the land" provision underscored a principle which eventually found its way to the Fifth and Fourteenth Amendments to the Constitution of the United States.

To equate the "law of the land" provision with the concept of "due process of law" is not without precedent. Parliament declared in 1354 (139 years after Magna Carta), "that no man of what estate or condition that he be, shall be put out of land or tenement, nor taken, nor imprisoned, nor disinherited, nor put to death, without being brought in answer by *due process of the law.*"

The origins of trial by jury extend to Continental sources earlier than Magna Carta, but it is Magna Carta that demands a judgment of peers, a demand which is based on one of the oldest principles of English law, namely that a man who is to be judged should be judged by his equals. Thus, a noble should not be judged by a vassal, and a vassal should not be judged by a subvassal. It is not unusual for writers on American constitutional law to equate trial by jury with the guarantees of Magna Carta. Mr. Justice Story, who served on our Supreme Court for thirty-three years beginning with 1812, in his *Commentaries*, a series of important legal essays, expressed the traditional view in these words:

It seems hardly necessary in this place to expatiate upon the antiquity or importance of the trial by jury in criminal cases. It was from very early times insisted on by our ancestors in the parent country, as the great bulwark of their civil and political liberties, and watched with an unceasing jealousy and solicitude. The right constitutes one of the fundamental articles of Magna Carta.

C. *The Lawyer of Colonial America*

Let me return to the lawyer's plight in Colonial days. In at least one of the colonies, even if the assistance of a lawyer were needed, he could not receive a fee for his services. We are told by one reliable source that "the authors of the Massachusetts Body of Liberties adopted in 1641, besides expressly permitting every litigant to plead his own cause, were careful to provide that, if unable to help himself and forced to employ an assistant, he was to give his counsel 'no fee or reward for his paines.' "[3] In the early years in the State of Maryland a local newsman rendered thanks "that there were no lawyers in that colony and no business to occupy such factious members of a community."

We are familiar with the role played by lawyers in the structuring of the Declaration of Independence and the work of its principal architect, Thomas Jefferson, a lawyer. We frequently refer to the number of lawyers who signed the Declaration of Independence. Similarly, without the handiwork of lawyers, the Constitution of the United States would not have been written in such enduring terms. What is not as well known is the tremendous contribution made by lawyers such as Madison, Alexander Hamilton and John Jay to the writing of the essays that constituted the Federalist Papers and which played an important role in the ratification of the Constitution by the States. Even more so, these essays have contributed immeasurably to an understanding of the Constitution and even to this day are referred to in looking to the background of provisions of the Constitution and the purposes and objectives the framers had in mind.

These essays constituting the *Federalist Papers* appeared in newspapers—four a week—from October 27, 1787 until the final one on May 28, 1788. It has been said that:

> what made it succeed was the fact that the three authors were persons who had been close to the heart of the great events of the past decade of independence and the struggle for nationhood. Jay had become the new country's most knowledgeable foreign affairs expert; Madison had taken such copious notes at the Philadelphia Convention that he would earn the title of "Father of the Constitution." As for Hamilton, his perception of the fundamental need for economic stability and centralized control of the essentials of defense, commerce and foreign relations, established the practical foundation for the American theory of government."[4]

[3]C. & M. BEARD, THE RISE OF AMERICAN CIVILIZATION 100-03 (1934).
[4]Swindler, *The Selling of the Constitution*, YEARBOOK 1980, SUPREME COURT HISTORICAL SOCIETY.

Thomas Jefferson described these *Federalist Papers* (he received his copies primarily from Madison) as "the best commentary on the principles of government which ever has been written."

I wonder if we ever pause to contemplate that none of the writers of the Federalist Papers had any means of foreseeing how the new government would work in practice. In reality, the pro-ratification advocates had to appeal to the delegates in the ratifying conventions to embrace the constitution more on the basis of faith than on any proven fact.

Still, despite the prominent part played by lawyers in the American Revolution and in the molding of independence from England, the legal profession did not have a proper acceptance after the war. There was an inclination to blame it for the miseries that the country endured. Acts were passed by some states that abolished the legal profession. The press, by and large, carried articles adverse to the lawyer and even as is done by some periodicals today, the lawyer was held up to public ridicule by the emphasizing of any shortcomings and a disregard of his contributions. Perhaps we should take note at this point of the unfortunate situation that then existed when young men joined the profession without the appropriate professional qualifications, and even worse, when some entered the profession without moral qualifications.

But better times came along. The profession reached a bright period of public leadership in the years from 1765 to 1820. Historians record that members of the profession showed qualities of independence of judgment and demonstrated pride and dignity in their responsibility of legal counseling. Lawyers participated in the shaping of social institutions, and all of this seemed to give the lawyer a new place in the sun.

The period from 1820 to 1860 has sometimes been referred to as the "Golden Age of American Law." It was then that law moved into a dominant role in the channeling of social affairs. Dean Roscoe Pound named this period the "Formative Era of American Law."

QUESTIONS AND ANSWERS

Leon Jaworski: I'll be happy to entertain any questions. I don't promise to answer them but we'll consider them anyway. Those that you propound, I would suggest that you do so clearly so that all in the room can understand. Otherwise, the answer may not be very meaningful. All right, yes, sir.

Male Voice: Mr. Jaworski, what's the most common criticism that you hear about the legal profession?

Jaworski: Well, first, let me tell you that I get an unusual number of letters and each hurts all over again. I've been receiving them for a long period of time; there are complaints about lawyers and some probably have more substance to them than I wish they had; but in some, of course, the complainant himself was at fault. I think that probably the most common complaint is that of foot dragging and not attending to matters. Lawyers will accept fees and then just simply don't perform, and that is absolutely inexcusable. I could sleep better at night if I were hungry—I mean real hungry—but had done everything that I could to help a poor person who had placed his trust in me—than to take his money and let this person believe that he is being helped when nothing is being done to help him, or when the matter is being delayed so long that the matter of help comes too late. And yet this happens, and it happens too often. I think the only way that this is going to be cured is for the younger generation of lawyers to address themselves to it and say, "We're going to put a stop to it." Let the law schools inculcate in them a belief, a strong belief, that this is absolutely essential in order for our profession to be regarded as it should be and for us especially to be entitled to the adjective of honorable; that we are an honorable profession. It's going to be necessary to do that, and I think it can be done. I think some improvement has been made in some places but there are way too many—still way too many grievances being filed against lawyers in our state and in other states, and there are too many delays in the handling of these grievances.

And that's another problem that needs attention. As you may know, there have already been steps taken in order to attempt to get grievance committees composed not only of lawyers but laymen as well, and it's true in our state. This is one of the concessions that we had to make in order to keep from being *sunsetted.* But this is very important to make sure that these grievance committees operate and can operate effectively. If they do, you'll find that there'll be a lot less of the fudging that has been going on and a lot less of some of the failures and some of the mishandlings that have been going on. We'll talk about that a little bit more in one of the future lectures. Next question.

Male Voice: We've taken so much from the English system; do you feel that it would promote better trial work if we somehow borrowed part of the English system in the barrister-and-solicitor type of system?

Jaworski: That's an excellent question. I want to say to you first, I wish you could witness some of the trials in England and be acquainted with the trial lawyers. In England, they have a dual system; they have the solicitors and they have the barristers. And for a man to become a barrister, which is a trial lawyer—he really has been subjected to a lot of good training; he spends a certain period of time in one of the inns,

9

either Lincoln's Inn or Gray's Inn of the Inner Temple or the Middle Temple, and there the barristers watch him, the members of the Queen's Council and others. And he gets his training there; this is where he really gets his training, right at the feet, so to speak, of outstanding barristers, trial lawyers. And they are, without exception, very, very able. They, of course, have a somewhat different system than we have. They strike at the heart of things there, more so than we do. And there's much to learn from their system. Now, we have, for a number of years, engaged in an exchange system with the English judges and the English barristers and some solicitors. We have brought them over to this country to study our system and give us suggestions and their thoughts, with respect to where we might undergird our efforts in our system. And we have, in turn, examined theirs for the purpose, not only of making suggestions, but also for the purpose of learning to see what we might find that was adaptable that we could use in our system. Of course, as you know, their trials come up much sooner than ours do; the delays there are not nearly so long, and the trials do not take that long, either. The trials there are quite speedy by comparison, and they do cut through a tremendous amount of so-called red tape. It's impressive, very impressive, and I think it's quite an education to watch a trial at an English court. The appellate courts—I just couldn't get over that—they're trying to do something about this—but, the House of Lords sits on appeal and there they sit, and you just keep talking and talking for several days at a time and that's your lawsuit. And they sit there and muse about it, you know, and ask a few questions now and then. And it's, again, I think, an antiquated, highly antiquated system; as much as I think of some of their trial techniques, I don't think too highly of their appellate system. So, there's much that—that they criticize in their own system and as much that they admire in what we do. I think our admiration of the English trial lawyer is largely because they are, almost without exception, really very, very good. Yes, sir, or yes, ma'am, for the next question—yes?

Male Voice: Mr. Jaworski, I was curious—you are most famous for—to us probably, for Watergate, and I have a question about that. In *U.S. v. Nixon*, James St. Clair relied heavily upon the Burr case where Thomas Jefferson refused to turn over private papers. How in the world—how did you distinguish Burr and—with President Nixon—what he did?

Jaworski: Well, it may have not been a good distinction. There may have not been a distinction at all, but at least the United States Supreme Court bought it. But you do make a good point. There were a number of circumstances that we talked about that were different in those days. And we certainly were not attempting to ignore the situation entirely, but when viewed in the light of what the political conditions and other circumstances were then, it was a matter that I don't believe deserved too much comment. And I would say this to you, that in the course of the argument, though the arguments were extended much longer than is normally the case—I might say considerably longer than is normally the case—the particular matter of the distinction in that case was never brought up by either the justices or by the lawyers. The fact remained that I thought we had a situation that was far different from anything else that had ever come up in the history of the United States of America or that ever confronted our judicial system. I thought that we were entitled to an examination of our matter entirely apart from what had ever occurred before because we had a completely new set of circumstances, a new set of facts; we had conditions that had not existed before. And after I get through answering that, I'm going to show you where we had that arising, not once but two or three times, and each time it had to stand on its own footing. We could not go with any particular precedent. Now, what do I mean? I'll tell you what I mean. I started early in the game feeling that it was very important that the court understand that here was a matter that was spawned in criminal conduct which put it apart from almost anything else that could be considered. Here was a situation where the President of the United States was in possession of information, and we demonstrated to the satisfaction of the court that it related to matters that had a setting, an environment of criminality— more than that. Not only was it necessary for us to have the facts so that we would know what the situation was; we also needed that information so that we could in fairness let the defendants who were coming to trial in that case—John Mitchell, Ehrlichman, Haldeman, the rest of them—have the benefit of whatever information there was if they wanted it. Now, there's no question but what some of the Justices on the Court, one or two of them in particular—let's see, one of them in particular—was rather eager that I not go into that, because, I think, that he would have rather not have faced that situation. It was not a happy one; it was an ugly one. It was one where we had to talk about the President of the United States; it was one where we had to talk about the fact that the grand jury had considered and named him as an unindicted co-conspirator and gave me the authority to name him as such and to file the specification delineating his conspiracy and his conduct in the conspiracy at any time that I felt it was necessary to do so. We had a ball game far different than any that had been played before. My position was simply this: that when you take all of these facts—and I have just hit some of those that were of the most significant in weight—when you take all of those and put them together, you have a factual situation where the Supreme Court of the United States could not, in my judgment, give rise to an unconstitutional approbation of executive privilege. It's been considered to have merit under certain circumstances that are readily recognized. But I painted, as best I could, the ugliness of this particular situation which I felt the Supreme Court of the United States would never permit to exist—would never say that in the light of that we will not give you that evidence, even in the light of that. So, let me just say to you that the emphasis that I put on the matter in my argument was that, and was not in trying to distinguish some situation that really grew out of a different set of circumstances than we had had. I did not feel the need of doing more than pointing to something that I believed in all of our annals of justice was singular and that under no circumstances could the court hand out a decision that would ignore the basic and fundamental truths of justice that prevailed in that situation. And apparently they felt that way about it. It was somewhat of a bold step, and yet I felt that it was a step that needed to be taken. I would say that your question, based purely upon the technical principles of law and the matter of distinguishing cases, is a very good question. And there is no question but that St. Clair used that in his brief and it may have even been used in an earlier brief filed by others. But it, to me, was not something that would have any controlling consequence or influence and for that reason we painted our own picture and laid it before the Court rather than worry about some of the others that we thought were dissimilar in their factual content.

II

The Constitution and the American Legal System

I want to return to Magna Carta at this point and its constitutional guaranty we enjoy today arguably traceable to the Great Charter. The overall impact of this magnificent English document is what arrests our attention at this hour.

We know that our liberties depend upon the existence of established and known rules of law that prescribe and limit the authority, and restrain the influence, of those to whom we have entrusted the power of government. We know from what we have examined historically today that Magna Carta announced the rule of law which is the foundation on which rests the entire edifice of Anglo-American constitutional liberties.

In these days our Constitution is universally admired. It is especially admired by our English friends across the ocean who possess constitutional rights but have no written constitution. They stand in awe of how well ours has functioned in turbulent times as well as in tranquil days.

In a volume entitled *The Lawyers* published by Wildy & Sons Ltd. of London, and written by Timothy Tyndale Daniell who is an English barrister at law of Gray's Inn, it is said that:

> The Courts have no power to declare an Act of Parliament unconstitutional merely because it takes away rights by Magna Carta or the Bill of Rights. The scandal of Watergate was uncovered and remedied in the United States, but in England the Government could have used its powers under the Official Secrets Acts to prevent any such revelations. Now the Parliament is "Supremo," and the Government supreme within it, the Englishman probably needs the protection for his liberties in a written constitution, as have been given the citizens of the United States. The price of liberty is eternal vigilance, and never must our pride in the Common Law, and its

13

own achievements, blind us to the need to modify, adapt and extend it anew to cope with the dangers of our modern age. . . .

A. *Watergate: A Demonstration of Constitutional Supremacy*

The English followed with avid interest the troublesome days that beset us a few years ago when the President of the United States—the most powerful man in the land—was bound in the chains of the Constitution. They observed the Supreme Court of the United States tell the President that the Court would interpret the Constitution and not he; that the Court would decide whether the Constitution required him to surrender evidence to be used in criminal proceedings and not he; that the Court would not permit him to read into the Constitution what was not there—neither would it permit him to take out of the Constitution what was there. What the Supreme Court of the United States said to the President of the United States can be summarized in these few words: "The rule of law—the spirit of constitutionalism—belongs to the people. It includes all, and it exempts none."

In the 1830's Alexis De Toqueville, a young statesman from France, came to our country to study our institutions, primarily those of a penal nature. He became engrossed in a study of American politics and particularly the workings of a democracy as was exemplified by our government in the 19th Century. His study of our institutions, our professions, our society and the parts of our system of government that comprised the whole has often been referred to by scholars as the greatest work on the polity and culture of our country. He studied the legal profession and the work of lawyers as a part of his endeavor and came to the conclusion that the authority this nation "has entrusted to members of the legal profession and the influence which these individuals exercise in the government is the most powerful existing security against the excesses of democracy."

In moving along with this historical review of the lawyer's status, note should be taken of the assessment of Supreme Court Justice Louis D. Brandeis in 1905:

> It is true that at the present time the lawyer does not hold that position with the people that he held 75 or indeed 50 years ago; but the reason is not lack of opportunity. We hear much of the 'corporation lawyer' and far too little of the 'people's lawyer.' The great opportunity of the American bar is and will be to stand again as it did in the past, ready to protect also the interests of the people.[5]

And just five years later President Woodrow Wilson referred to a "new type of lawyer" in these words:

[5] *The Opportunity and the Law*, 39 AM. L. REV. 55 (1905).

A new type of lawyer has been created; and that new type has come to be the prevailing type. Lawyers have been sucked into the maelstrom of the business system of the country. That system is highly technical and highly specialized. It is divided into distinct sections and provinces, each with particular legal problems of its own. Lawyers, therefore, everywhere that business has thickened and had a large development, have become experts in some special technical field. They do not practice law. They do not handle the general, miscellaneous interest of society. They are not general counselors of right and obligation. They do not bear the relation to the business of their neighborhoods that the family doctor bears to the health of the community in which he lives. They do not concern themselves with the universal aspects of society.[6]

And only five years ago, then Secretary of State Henry Kissinger referred to the work of lawyers in the current century in these words:

In this century lawyers have been consistently at the center of our diplomacy, providing many of our ablest Secretaries of State and diplomats, and often decisively influencing American thinking about foreign policy.[7]

B.   *The Lawyer's Role in Watergate: Creating & Unraveling the Tangle*

Following Watergate it was not uncommon for members of the news media to ask me of my reaction to the unusual number of lawyers involved in the Watergate scandal. This is in line with the usual twitting that the news media enjoys doing whenever lawyers have fallen in disrepute. My first reaction to one or two of these initial inquiries was simply to point out that these lawyers, although vaccinated as such, were not engaged in the actual practice of law—with few exceptions—and that they were really not a part of our ongoing profession. I realized, however, that this was a very poor explanation and really not even an extenuating circumstance to the charge. On reflection, I did deem it necessary to concede that this was a dark spot on the escutcheon of the legal profession and that it would be a cross we would have to bear. There was no excuse for so many holding law licenses to become implicated in such a deplorable series of events. What I later concluded as a fair reaction to the inquiry was to concede the stigma—then ask the critics to acknowledge the work of members of the legal profession in unravelling the facts and in bringing about a fair and just investigation. The point I underscored was that there are two sides to the ledger and that both sides should be taken into account.

[6]Address by Woodrow Wilson, 1910 Annual Meeting of the American Bar Association (Aug. 30, 1910).
[7]Address by Henry A. Kissinger, 1975 Annual Meeting of the American Bar Association (Aug. 11, 1975).

Perhaps it is well to digress at this moment to mention that a number of the lawyers so involved were disbarred—others involved to a lesser degree were given different but appropriate disciplinary punishment. It would interest you to know that, without exception, the serving of time in a penal institution as a felon did not bother these individuals nearly as much as the loss of their license to practice law. Several of the disbarred discussed this problem with me, and I was impressed with their deep grief in the loss of their right to practice their chosen profession. A number of them have since petitioned the authorities in their states for reinstatement. Two have been readmitted, the most recent being Egil (Bud) Krogh of the State of Washington, who was convicted of conspiring illegally to enter a doctor's office in search of records in the Ellsberg matter, in violation of civil rights. I supported his petition for reinstatement because of his early confession of guilt, his remorse and his subsequent cooperation with us.

Perhaps the best way to wrap up this part of the lecture is to quote what was said by Edward G. Ryan of Wisconsin, a great lawyer who practiced with rare distinction in the middle part of the 19th Century. He put it this way:

> The legal profession has done many bad things and has produced many bad men; but it is a glorious old profession, and I love it and am proud of it. It may do in these days of demagogues to denounce it; but I say now and always, here and elsewhere, what all history proves, that there was seldom a great stride made in human progress on which the bar was not a moving power. It is an honorable profession, an independent profession.

Of one thing I am certain—a fact that does not admit of argument. There is no way in our system of government that justice can be attained without the conscientious labor of the lawyer. And what is "justice"? I will let Daniel Webster define it as he did in September of 1845:

> Justice is the great interest of man on earth. It is the ligament which holds civilized beings and civilized nations together, wherever her temple stands, and so long as it is duly honored, there is a foundation for social security, general happiness, and the improvement and progress of our race. And whoever labors on this edifice with usefulness and distinction, whoever clears its foundations, strengthens its pillars, adorns its entablatures, or contributes to raise its august dome still higher in the skies, connects himself, in name and fame, and character, with that which is and must be as durable as the frame of human society.

QUESTIONS AND ANSWERS

Leon Jaworski: With that we'll end the second series of lectures and we'll be open to questions. Questions do not necessarily have to bear upon today's lecture, of course. There may be something that has occurred to you since we met yesterday and I'm open to such questions as you wish to propound. All right, there's a question right there.

Male Voice: Despite the taint on the profession that Watergate brought, looking prospectively, can the profession survive this taint? And, if so, what steps would be most beneficial to that effect?

Jaworski: I believe that the profession has done—that is the American Bar Association, has done and I'm certain that some of the state bar associations have also done the same thing—by way of trying to tighten up our code of professional responsibility. I think that perhaps the best thing that happened was the successful prosecution of these lawyers and the fact that they have had to serve time. And if every lawyer knew how these have borne an agony and a heartbreak and a realization of the great torture that comes to one who loses his law license, who's been disbarred, then I believe that every lawyer would think twice before he would commit any transgression on our moral responsibilities. But the danger, of course, when you have an incident such as Watergate, which of course was really so noticeable and its impact so great because it was so unusual—it had such terrific dimensions—but when you have something like that, the danger is of everybody rushing in, to want to have regulations, statutes, all kinds of barriers and all sorts of restraints as to make sure that none of these things can happen again. And, of course, it all goes back also to there not only being laws, there not only being restraints—administrative, legislative—but also on what the profession itself is going to do about it. This is really the important thing. This is the great factor and the factor that I hope someday we will find that we can applaud. I do think that the profession has been addressing itself to some of these problems. I think the law schools and the professions are going to have to really get behind these particular problems in our profession. If that is done, then we can reduce some of the failures that we experience, some of the things that the public can properly point to, that the news media can properly relate and carry in their columns. These matters will be reduced to a minimum and once we've done that, we will have helped ourselves tremendously and upgraded our profession to no end. All right. Next question.

Male Voice: With your permission, sir, I would like to follow up on that first question and simply ask—Have we, with the ruling in the *U.S. v. Nixon*, approached a potentially dangerous situation with regards to the constitutional doctrine of separation of powers?

Jaworski: I don't think so. Now, you'll notice that the Court was very careful in its opinion to recognize that there are times when the president does have the right to exercise executive privilege. As a matter of fact, the opinion may well stand for one of the strongest expressions that has ever come out of the United States Supreme Court recognizing the existence of executive privilege. But, it has to be confined to certain situations that are acceptable and are recognized. Now, I'll say this: that the strong issue before the Court in that case was whether you're going to let the United States president, a president of our country, construe the Constitution or whether you're going to let the court construe the Constitution. Now, it came to a point, really, where it would have been disastrous, in my way of thinking—and I'm making allowance for my own prejudice in the situation—it would have been disastrous if the United States Supreme Court had not said, "We're going to construe the Constitution, and we're going to tell the president what the Constitution says. And we're not going to let the president tell us what the Constitution says; we're going to tell him and he's going to accept it." And the United States Supreme Court had done that before. They've told more than one president what the Constitution would permit and what it wouldn't permit. You'll be learning in constitutional law of a number of cases where presidents have undertaken to do certain things and the Supreme Court has said, "No! It can't be done." The Supreme Court, since way back yonder—you can see *Marbury v. Madison*, the Supreme Court has told Congress that it cannot do certain things. So then it's told the executive; it's told Congress. And it has made it very clear that it is going to be the arbiter of what the Constitution permits. Now, you know, for a long period of time in the early days of the Supreme Court, one doubted just how strong this branch of government was going to be. Would it really be a very strong and effective and potent branch of our government? As time went on, as we all noticed, it has become a tremendously powerful branch of our government. It has been referred to by some writers and some authors as the least dangerous branch. I think in the Watergate days that it showed itself to have to be the most illustrious branch. But, this is the way one reacts when he happens to come out all right. But this is the best answer that I can give you. Yes, there was a question over here. Yes, Sir.

Male Voice: This is another Watergate-related question, Mr. Jaworski. What did you think of John Connally's advice to President Nixon that Mr. Nixon should take his tapes out on the White House lawn and have a bonfire?

Jaworski: Well, regardless of what John Connally's advice was or his views were—let me discuss that with you a moment. Really, there was a time when President Nixon could have destroyed these tapes and I

18

think the American people would have accepted it. There would have been an uprising of protests on the part of many; I think he would have survived it and I think he would have gotten by with it. Actually, bear in mind now, that this is government property; the government paid for it—may not have been a vast amount of money involved; that has nothing to do with it. But the government paid for the installation of the system; the government paid for the tapes themselves and the government paid for their operation—employees who operate. So, it would, in a sense, have been and constituted the destruction of government property which, of course, is a federal offense. I think if Mr. Nixon had taken the position before the people early in the game—not after things got so bad, but early in the game—that he, because of the existence of very important and highly significant and secretive communications on these tapes that affected the welfare of our nation, the security of our nation and our dealings with the heads of other states, that he had to take these tape recordings and destroy them now that it had become known that they existed, I think he would have gotten by. I think he would have gotten by with it, but he waited too long. And having waited as he did, the people would never have bought it. As a matter of fact, if he had destroyed the tape recordings later on, I think he would have been impeached overnight. So that's the difference in the timing of what one may do. I want to get back to discussing one matter that I said I probably would touch on and I didn't when I started talking about the United States Supreme Court case. And I think it was in answer to your question. Remember that we were plowing new ground. We had no law books to go to; there was no precedent that we could find anywhere that really told us what we could do. I think really that the turning point in Watergate was not so much the decision of the United States Supreme Court itself—I think it was very important. If we had lost that case, I would have just packed up and stolen out of town like the Arabs, very frankly, because there wouldn't have been anything else to do. But I think the big turning point was when there was something done for the first time in history and that was when we commenced a judicial proceeding to get the Court's permission to turn over secret grand jury testimony to the House Judiciary Committee sitting in impeachment—considering articles of impeachment of the President of the United States. Here we were with a lot of evidence that we had kept completely secret. I couldn't talk about it; neither could the grand jurors; neither could anybody else. We couldn't pass it on to anyone voluntarily. We couldn't let anyone be privy to what we had, and yet it was very, very strong, powerful, and effective testimony—evidence of one kind and another. We were holding that and having to hold it under wraps. And the House Judiciary Committee was sitting there and not having anything; very frankly, they were spinning their wheels. They weren't getting anywhere and they were coming to me and crying on my shoulder, and there wasn't anything that I could do because I was bound not to reveal what we had. I couldn't tell them anything that we had, much less give them anything. So we initiated this proceeding, and the whole purpose of it was to get the courts to authorize doing something that we could not do. And that is to pass on to the House Judiciary Committee the grand jury testimony that we had. And we prepared a grand jury report and it was rewritten in my office I don't know how many times. I rewrote it myself the last two or three times. And the whole purpose of rewriting it so often was to get the maximum of information—we called that the road map, where we took it chronologically and suggested just exactly what happened, when it happened, what was done, and what the testimony showed—the grand jury testimony, which was all a part of our road map—supporting the map as an exhibit—the tape recordings that we had as an exhibit. We took all of that as a grand jury report and asked the court to permit it being passed to the House Judiciary Committee. And this was the first time in history; that just had not been done before. I think the central key to the entire success of that rested in our doing it on a basis of not accusing anyone with it. What we did is simply carried forward what the facts were, passed them on, not making an effort to interpret them, not making any sort of an effort to construe or to say what we thought it showed and let it be completely non-accusative. And that went to the House Judiciary Committee and they were in business. Now, that case, as you remember, was laid before Sirica to begin with and was argued. We prevailed. It was then appealed to the Circuit Court of Appeals and argued; we prevailed. And then for some reason, they decided to quit and did not take an appeal to the Supreme Court. And then the entire matter went to the House Judiciary Committee. That permitted that committee to really understand what it was all about and to obtain evidence on which they could begin to consider their work. This is the turning point in that entire unhappy and unfortunate affair that has been overlooked in history. I think, probably, one of these days it will be dug up—talked about more than it has been heretofore.

Male Voice: Mr. Jaworski, haven't you used a form of plea bargaining in your own Watergate prosecution? Do you feel that plea bargaining is being overused in the general judiciary?

Jaworski: Plea bargaining, if used properly—and I want to thank you for giving me a chance to express myself on this—if it's used properly, it is one of the finest, best vehicles that's available in our whole processes of law. Now, it depends upon those who engage in plea bargaining as to whether it's used properly. Now here, let's just take Watergate as an example because I have no apologies, and I'm always proud to point to it as what I think was appropriate plea bargaining. Here were men who finally caved in and who said to us, "all right, we're willing to tell you all about it." We said, "O.K., we'll take your plea, but what we will do is, we're insisting that you will not be immune from our proceeding against you for perjury if we find that you have lied. Now, before we will take your plea, you're going to have to go before the grand jury and you tell your story. If you're willing to tell it truthfully and let it be tested, then we'll take your plea. What will we do in return? We will charge you with a felony. The judge will send you to the penitentiary—for how long, that's his decision; that's not ours. We will not charge you with other felonies that we could charge." And I want to tell you very frankly whether a man plea bargains or whether he doesn't, I don't think we give him very much by charging him with only one felony. A man who has been convicted of a felony—what difference does it make if you add another one to it or not? To people of that kind, there is absolutely no purpose in saying that they should serve one year instead of six months, for instance, if everything has been done that can possibly be done for society by sending him to the penitentiary. Lawyers lost their licenses and so on. Now, plea bargaining can be abused just as any other process of law can be abused. And I have been absolutely amazed at how some jump on plea bargaining as saying, "Well, you know, maybe it's a dirty process," when it is one of the most useful, provided that it is used correctly, processes there is in our whole system of justice. The American Bar Association had the very finest minds in the whole country study it over a period of several years: judges, lawyers, prosecutors, defenders—everybody was brought in, and they came out with a strong recommendation of its use. The trouble arises when it's misused. But there is no process of justice that can't be misused. And when it is misused, of course, it rears its ugly head. So, all I can say to you is that had it not been for the process of plea bargaining, we could never have unraveled Watergate. There wouldn't have been any way of doing it, because the way we were able to do it, to finally get the information that led us to be able to indicate what tapes we wanted and were able to obtain, these eventually were because we could pinpoint from the testimony that we got from these people who plea bargained precisely what happened at what date. Now, if we hadn't been able to do that, if fellows like Jeb Magruder and John Dean, Herb Kalmbach, Egil Krogh, and several others hadn't folded and hadn't plea bargained with us, we would never have been able to proceed with it. O.K., there was someone who—yes, you had your hand up.

Male Voice: If you could scratch a line from the Constitution or add a sentence, what would you make it?

Jaworski: Right now I have been dealing with the Constitution. I don't know what I would add to it. Well, I do know one thing I probably would change, and we get a little bit into the political field. I'm becoming more and more disenchanted over the idea of the terms for the presidency. I don't mind saying that it's been my observation for a number of years that the president in the second term just does not operate as well as he does the first term. And if I were to do it today, I would either hold his sentence to a six-year term or to a four-year term. And it may surprise you to know that I'm almost more committed to the idea of a four-year term than I am a six-year term. So that's about the only thing that comes to mind at the moment that I would change. Now, we are not talking, of course, about E.R.A. because whatever needs to be done along that line to give our lady friends what they feel they should have, I certainly would not oppose for a moment. I don't like to see the Constitution amended often, very frankly. I think we should steer away from it, and if congressional action will take care of something, let's do that; let's not run to the Constitution and start cutting it up. I just fear the idea of constitutional conventions, for instance. The Constitution has done a great job for us. Part of it, of course, is due to the very fine task the Supreme Court has done in interpreting it. There have been failures, of course, but, gee, there's nothing that is more highly regarded and more worshipped among those who have a free system and believe in the rule of law than our Constitution. So, I don't want to tamper with it.

III

The Adversary System

I want to talk with you about the adversary system as it is conducted in our land, as it is viewed by others, and my own beliefs of its efficacy in promoting justice. To get to a common understanding of what we mean by the adversary system, I adopt the explanation given by my friend, Geoffrey N. Hazard, Jr., in his volume on "Ethics in the Practice of Law."

> The adversary system is a procedure for trial of civil and criminal cases, and is the characteristic form of trial procedure in common law countries. Its essential feature is that a decision is made by judge, or judge with jury, who finds the facts and determines the law from submissions made by partisan advocates on behalf of the parties. The system contrasts with what is generally called the inquisitorial system, used in countries of the civil law tradition such as France and Germany. In this system of trial, which might less invidiously be called the interrogative system, the judge determines the law and finds the facts by his own active investigation and inquiries at trial.

I take my position with my colleagues in the American College of Trial Lawyers, a preeminent organization of trial lawyers in this country. Professor Matt Dawson of your Law School is a member of this College, having been admitted when he was an active trial lawyer prior to coming to the law school. What we said in a resolution unanimously adopted by my fellow Regents of the College in March of 1979 is that "[f]rom its roots in the origins of the common law, through the entire life of this nation, the adversary system has evolved into the best and fairest method of justice known anywhere in the world."

I have never opposed the idea of progressiveness and have never favored a dragging of feet when improvements in the administration of justice can be made. I am not happy with all phases of the system as it operates today. I doubt that I would ever find it to be in full accord with my concepts of how the machinery of justice should operate. But this is beside the point. One does not discard a system that has basic values simply because it has some imperfections. And to dispense with the adversary system, in my view, is to dispense with a tried and reasonably true means of achieving justice. I am agreeable with going along with the advocacy of realigning our profession into the advancements of modern society to whatever degree is reasonable, so long as it does not dispense with a basic value such as the adversary system.

It is largely because of the adversary system that the lawyer's influence upon the development of law in our nation has been so profound. Law is not an exact science as Lord Halsbury reminded us. But regardless of its shortcomings at times, it is the adversary system that enables it to deal effectively and in most instances fairly with the rights of individuals. The lawyer's role in our legal system cannot be overestimated. It is his work, his research, his resourcefulness, his many hours of thought and study, and frequently his foresight and his grasp of the problems of society that make the laws under which we live. Oftentimes, the judge merely adopts the product of a lawyer's labor. The better the lawyer does his work, the better will be the contribution made to the body of law and the more rewarding will the effort be to mankind. There is hardly a great judicial decision that does not have as its forerunner the careful and brilliant work of advocates.

The law cannot be static. It must march with the progress of a civilization. Who is to forge the continuous expansion and review of legal principles if it is not to be done largely by the lawyer through the adversary system? No less an authority than Lord Denning, the Master of the Rolls of England to whom I referred earlier, recently stated that "the principles of law laid down in the 19th Century—however suited for social conditions of that time—are not suited to the social necessities and social opinion of the 20th Century." He added that, "they should be molded and shaped to meet the needs and opinions of today."

A.   *The System's Weaknesses*

The legal profession must find an answer to the high cost of litigation which has reached alarming proportions, and unless checked, will make litigation prohibitive except for the wealthy and for large business interests. Once this plight is reached, our system of justice will have failed, and other means of settling disputes are certain to be legislated and resorted to.

Attorneys fees are not the only burden. The cost of depositions and investigations has increased sharply. Expert witness fees—transportation costs and other costs of preparation for trial have increased substantially in recent years. Congestions in courts and other causes of delay add to the cost of litigating and suggest to the parties that quicker ways of determining rights and settling disputes should be found. It behooves the legal profession to address itself to these adverse conditions and to come up with answers that will overcome these soft spots and thus preserve the adversary system.

The adversary system has been studied in recent years by numerous groups and individual legal scholars. In 1975 the American Assembly, together with the American Bar Association, conducted a study into matters pertaining to the law and the changing society. One of the studies related to the adversary system. Here are the comments resulting from that study:

> Our principal system of adjudication is the adversary system. In that system, the truth, in the sense of relevant facts accurately determined, is vitally important for the rational administration of justice. Too often our adversary techniques conceal or distort the truth rather than promote its discovery. The legal profession should consider and explore appropriate modifications of adversary procedures for the purpose of better determining the truth, and should formulate ethical prescriptions embracing a higher professional duty to seek the truth.
>
> Lawyers are administrators of justice as well as advocates of clients. Lawyers and those training for the practice of law have an affirmative responsibility to nurture justice and truth.

With these observations I agree in the main. The fact remains, however, that in my judgment a better system has not been devised. The point that this study makes is one I share—that it behooves the legal profession to do whatever it can to strengthen the weak links that appear in the chain of the adversary system—weaknesses for which the lawyers themselves frequently are responsible.

I cannot accept the criticism that the adversary system fails, because too often the outcome depends on the superior ability of one counsel over the other. In my experience, this is not the criterion as a rule. I do not deny that it is at times. What usually determines capable performance in the courtroom is the thoroughness of preparation, both of the facts and the law—and not native ability. I have seen trial lawyers of considerable stature and reputation do a very ordinary job in the courtroom due to lack of adequate preparation. I have also seen lawyers not naturally blessed in advocacy talent perform admirably because of the thoroughness of their preparation.

Neither do I accept the dim view some take of jury trials as part of the adversary system. Except in the most unusual of factual situations, I would never waive a jury. Although my trial work was in general litigation involving a large variety of cases, I also handled a few defense insurance cases involving automobile collisions and malpractice. Even in the latter, I preferred a jury. I learned that I could reason with my jurors—at least with most of them. I believed that if I could not persuade them with the right and justice of my side of the case, I should have no expectation of winning.

It is not that I distrust judges. Some of the judges before whom I frequently tried jury cases were friends of mine—still, I preferred not to waive a jury—not even at the court's suggestion. I became convinced that the judge's view was more likely to be affected, subconsciously, by predilections; that some of his ideas and notions were likely to be set in concrete and would control his ultimate judgment. I wanted in the trier of facts men and women with open and uncolored minds. I did not always get a complete panel to meet these specifications but those instances were the exception. Perhaps my strong leanings in favor of jury trials were bent by an experience in a nonjury trial in my early years in the practice. When His Honor announced the judgment of the court, I thought that he had fleeced my client. Fortunately, the case did not involve much, but it set my unalterable course in future trials. I do not mean to leave the impression that of the many juries to which I tried my cases each left me in a celebrative mood. I do mean to say that in my entire experience there was no jury that I felt had wronged my client— save one. The exception involved the conduct of a foreman of the jury who had misled the other jurors. I was able to set that verdict aside due to irreconcilable findings.

This phase of the discussion should end with the statement made by the eminent Lord Chief Justice of England, Lord Widgery, with whom I have spent many hours in conversation and in social enjoyment. In the lecture that he delivered on "The Compleat Advocate," he said this:

> The quality of the trial lawyer is not primarily dependent on his basic training in law school, or on his having an exceptionally high intelligence quotient. The essential requirements are discipline and dedication.

Recent news reports described the dramatic turn of events in the trial of a priest charged with several offenses of robbery. Each victim's sworn testimony positively identified the accused, who steadfastly denied his guilt. Before the trial was completed, the real robber appeared through his attorney and admitted guilt to each of the crimes. There was a resemblance in the physical appearance of the priest and that of the robber. Suppose the guilty person had not come forward. "Unmistakable" identification having been made, justice would likely have miscarried. Do such instances condemn the system?

Notwithstanding practical shortcomings and failures, basically our system of justice is as good, if not better, than any in existence. How well the system works depends primarily on the effective and conscientious conduct of the participants. Justice under law is achieved by a chain of events—each link must do its part. The investigators must be experienced and fair-minded, the prosecutors conscientious and not swayed by undue zeal or ambition, the witnesses must be upright and truthful, the judge learned and unbiased. Thus, the judicial process is composed of a number of integral and indispensable parts, none of which must falter if there is to be justice under law.

B. *The Lawyer as Guardian of Equality*

Why not say "equal justice under law"—the words so boldly chiseled over the entrance to the United States Supreme Court Building? What the third branch of government is saying is that this is the Court's aim—to grant to all an equal brand of justice under law. Laudable as is the goal, in actual practice there is no equal justice under law. The words are aphoristic, and why?

The process is the handiwork of human beings—from beginning to end—individuals possessed of frailties—of strengths and of weaknesses, of prejudices and biases, of foibles and of faulty judgments.

The trials of a violent act in the West, followed by one under identical circumstances in the East, end in widely disparate results. The offense charged is the same—the witnesses tell the same story—jurors are selected in the same manner—and the judge presides fairly. Still, in the one case the accused is freed—in the other he is sent to prison. Such happenings have occurred numerous times. Inconsistency in the outcome of comparable civil cases also plagues the system.

Much is made by critics of instances where jury verdicts appear to have gone awry, when little is said of the countless instances in which juries, by careful and painstaking service, have undergirded our system of justice. A society does not toss overboard a long proven system simply because of occasional failures—rather it strives to correct existing shortcomings.

The United States Supreme Court's greeting over its portals is not to be literally construed as an ironclad warranty. It must be viewed in the light of human characteristics and experiences. The nine men who compose the court, each with predilections of his own before he became a justice, and still possessed of them, are motivated by human emotions, beliefs and convictions. Two justices reading the same briefs, hearing the same arguments and studying the same precedents reach diametrically opposite views. Constitutional rights denied to a litigant twenty-five years ago are granted to another litigant this year.

27

Justice Brandeis would speak about a living constitution and of its guarantees being adaptable to a changing world. In his dissents he spoke out against the Supreme Court assuming the character of a super-legislature. Justice Holmes rebelled against stretching the due process clause to the limit of the sky. But the Warren Court paid little attention to him. Harlan Stone in a case involving the Agricultural Adjustment Act said: "the only check upon our own exercise of power is our own sense of self-restraint." That restraint has not been too evident in recent times. It has been pointed out, correctly it appears, that Charles Evans Hughes was destined to adapt the Constitution to the "bewildering requirements of an economic and social transition."

What the Supreme Court holds out to all those who come before it is an assurance that the court is prepared to grant, and will strive to grant, equal justice under law to all, regardless of who the litigants may be. That this is the Court's earnest intention is not to be doubted. The many 5-to-4 decisions in the Court's history, the numerous changes of direction in important social issues and constitutional interpretations, indicate no guarantee of such a result.

Nevertheless, we must keep embracing the doctrine of equal justice under law, point to it and praise it. Still more importantly, we must resolve to discharge our own responsibilities in the process of justice, uprightly and effectively, thereby bringing us closer and closer to reaching what may be the unreachable equal justice under law. Every citizen, from witness and juror to the Chief Justice of the United States and his colleagues can help brighten the process.

In appraising our criminal justice system, there comes to mind Winston Churchill's definition of a democratic form of government. He referred to a democracy as being "the worst form of government there is, except for all others that have been tried."

The American Bar Association, the American College of Trial Lawyers, and other organizations to which lawyers belong remind us in their codes that a lawyer should not decline to undertake the defense of a person accused of a crime or the representation of a litigant in a civil cause because his conduct, his reputation, or the position he happens to occupy may be the subject of public unpopularity or clamor. These and other organizations tell the members of the legal profession that in the discharge of the duty a lawyer owes his client, the lawyer should not be deterred by any real or fancied fear of falling into disfavor with others or suffering public unpopularity.

The root of the problem—the reason lawyers are sometimes deterred—is the public's misconception of the role of the lawyer. Throughout my years of practice, I have found laymen assuming that it is the lawyers' responsibility to pass judgment on the client's rights and that if he suspects the client may be in the wrong, the lawyer should not represent him. This false assumption is allowed to exist without much effort on the part of anyone to correct it.

Erskine, in his famous defense of Thomas Paine in 1792, made the point in these eloquent words:

> From the moment that any advocate can be permitted to say, that he will, or will not stand between the Crown and the subject arraigned in the court where he daily sits to practice, from that moment the liberties of England are at an end. If the advocate refuses to defend, from what he may think of the charge or of the defence, he assumes the character of the Judge; nay, he assumes it before the hour of judgment.

In 1871, the Court of Exchequer of England observed:

> A man's rights are to be determined by the court, and not by his attorney or counsel. It is for want of remembering this that foolish people object to lawyers saying that they will advocate a case against their own opinion. A client is entitled to say to his counsel, 'I want your advocacy and not your judgment. I prefer the judgment of the court.'

Examples of public misunderstanding in our land of the lawyer's duty to represent unpopular clients and causes—and the willingness of lawyers to ignore clamor while they go ahead and do their job—antedate even the American Revolution.

In the Boston Massacre of 1770, several Americans were killed by British soldiers. It was charged that this was coldblooded murder; that Captain John Preston of the British Army had ordered his troops to fire. Local feeling ran high against the British soldiers involved and especially against Captain Preston. There was great clamor for his trial and execution.

A friend of the Captain's came to John Adams, attorney and leader in the American cause. The friend said that the Captain's life was in great danger. He insisted that, in fact, Captain Preston had not ordered his troops to fire. A group of a hundred or more Americans had gathered and had thrown clubs and brickbats at the soldiers. A soldier fired his musket accidentally and in the melee and excitement that followed other soldiers fired too.

Soon, indignant Americans crowded at the entrance to Adams' office demanding that he tell them whether he would represent Captain Preston. Amid threats against him, John Adams replied that he expected to defend not only the Captain, but the soldiers charged as well. With that, he slammed the door to his office and went to work preparing his case. Captain Preston was acquitted and so were some of the soldiers.

One account tells how, when Adams made his argument to the jury, he said, "The law no passion can disturb. 'Tis void of desire and fear, lust and anger." Then, moving closer to the jury, he argued, "The law on the one hand is inexorable to the cries and lamentations of the prisoners. On the other hand, it is deaf, deaf as an adder, to the clamors of the populace."

When asked why he defended these British soldiers, Adams answered, "If I can but be the instrument of preserving one life, his blessing and tears of transport shall be a sufficient consolation for me, for the contempt of all mankind."

This stout-hearted lawyer was criticized, shunned, and threatened, but after the popular outcry subsided and men's thoughts returned to reason, Adams was elected to the House of Representative of the Commonwealth of Massachusetts. Afterward, he was the first Vice-President and then second President of the United States.

Judge Harold Medina, while a practicing attorney, was appointed to defend a man charged with treason during World War II. Our country was in a death struggle with the Nazi tyranny. The defendant, a German-born naturalized American citizen, was charged with aiding German saboteurs who had slipped ashore on Long Island in 1942 from a submarine. It is difficult to conceive of a more despised person to defend in the midst of a ferocious war.

There was a serious question of the man's guilt. The Constitution requires specific proof, including two witnesses to the overt act, to convict a person of treason, and Medina made certain that the law was meticulously applied. We are told by Judge Medina's biographer that "[t]hroughout the trial people sometimes shrank from contact with Medina as he entered court, as if they feared contamination, and once, as he made his way through the crowded courtroom toward the counsel table, a man leaned toward him and deliberately spat in his face."

In the summation to the jury, Medina minutely covered every detail of the case, using almost twenty thousand words. When the defense and the prosecution rested and the judge had charged the jury, he turned to Medina. Judge Goddard praised him generously for his willing performance during the trial and for doing so at the court's request, without pay.

Medina stood thoughtfully through this praise, and then did what was perhaps the hardest thing he ever had to do. "Judge Goddard," he replied, "I do not wish to appear ungracious, but I must respectfully except to what you have said. I do not believe that you had any right to tell the jury that I have been defending this man as assigned counsel." The case went to the United States Supreme Court on appeal twice. The second time, the Court's ruling caused the charge of treason to be dismissed.

I observed with admiration the work of American officers—lawyers in civilian life—appointed to defend the accused in war crimes trials held in Germany following World War II. Some of the crimes they were charged with were more barbarous than any in history. Yet American lawyers, to their everlasting credit, fought vigorously and tenaciously, but with propriety and dignity, to make certain that the accused had fair trials.

These instances I have mentioned are but a few of the many in which American trial lawyers have proved themselves worthy of their traditions, turning a deaf ear to intimidation and criticism, and defending unpopular causes courageously. Nor need we turn the pages of history to a century ago, or decades ago, for striking illustrations of the conduct of lawyers in similar situations today.

Let me add, too, that the accolade here intended by me for the lawyer who represents fearlessly those held in public scorn implies that he will resort only to ethical and legitimate means in the course of the representation. John Adams illustrated this point when he was solicited to defend Captain Preston. His words of caution were direct and unmistakable when he said that Captain Preston must expect from him "no art or address, no sophistry or prevarication . . . nor anything more than fact, evidence and law would justify."

It is truly disquieting to observe in these days a growing tendency of some of the most capable members of the bar to shun the acceptance of representation of those in public disfavor. When entering the profession, a lawyer does not engage in a popularity contest, but he does assume a special creed—as the late Mr. Justice Jackson put it—to "safeguard every man's right to a fair trial."

The greatest reward that flows to a lawyer is not measured in riches, social position, or popularity. Rather, it comes as an unseen, intangible inner satisfaction that emanates from the faithful discharge of duty. This is truly the lawyer's highest form of compensation.

C. *The Lawyer as Preserver of Laws*

Recently I read an article on "New Orleans After the Victory." It referred to the conduct of Andrew Jackson—also known as "Old Hickory." Jackson was thought to have been somewhat high-handed in his actions. He kept the militia under arms and New Orleans under martial law at a time when it was thought by public officials no longer to be necessary. It is said that once the immediate danger was past, the Governor and the Legislature showed a marked resentment of Jackson's high-handed ways. Now let me quote to you the importance of what followed:

> Out of this situation grew a series of unpleasant incidents, culminating in a fine of $1,000 imposed on Jackson by a Federal Judge for contempt of court. Jackson bore himself with dignity in the courtroom and paid the fine. He quelled a popular demonstration in his favor, advising his friends to recognize the supremacy of the law.

This is the only course a good American interested in preserving the rule of law should follow. It is the only course a lawyer, true to his oath, can conscientiously follow.

A brief panorama of what has occurred in our borders within recent months unfolds thus: despite the existence of laws that forbid policemen, firemen, teachers and other public employees to strike and the issuance of court orders restraining them from continuing their conduct and ordering their return to work, both laws and court decrees have been ignored and wantonly flouted. In one of our larger cities, in violation of state law, policemen and firemen both went on strike and disregarded the court order to return to their duties. In another city, striking firemen watched an entire block of buildings burn down without out a one of them lending a helping hand to control the fire that threatened the business district and could well have been ruinous to a major portion of that city. In still another city, striking teachers formed picket lines around schools to which children were reporting for classes and where quickly assembled substitute teachers were undertaking to carry on. I watched this on television. To my dismay, here were large groups of teachers whose obligations were to instill into these young folk, most of them of a highly impressionable age, concepts of good citizenship, jeering, shouting epithets and engaging in various disorders, and generally acting like ruffians and rogues. Some of them were arrested, sentenced for contempt of court and confined, where, as jailbirds, they were exemplifying citizenship behavior for their students to emulate.

In most localities in this land, if not in all of them, a police officer takes an oath that he will abide by and support the law. When he violates a state law prohibiting him from striking and when he disregards a court order directing him to cease his striking activities and return to his duties, he is not only flouting the law but contributing to its erosion. Picture this—an officer of the law who has taken an oath to uphold the law and who has been arresting people and charging them with a variety of law violations overnight becoming a law breaker himself.

I am not at all unsympathetic to working conditions that some officers, firemen and teachers, for example, have to endure. I am not at all unsympathetic with the low and sometimes inadequate compensation they receive. For years I have been advocating that these segments of our society, so important to the maintenance of a high level of social conduct, receive appropriate compensation and enjoy satisfactory working conditions. But they must remember that the city council is available to them—the state legislature is available to them—the polls are available to them—the open forum for an airing of their problems is available to them. All of these serve as proper places of resort for remedial action. Finally, if they find compensation and other factors unbearable, they can resign in honor. Where the right to strike is not forbidden by law, legislative or judicial, and is conducted in orderly fashion, society accepts and respects the exercise of that right—and I would not want for one moment to criticize the invocation of that right.

It is the obligation of the lawyer to rise in protest against such violation, and I hope to see the day when lawyers *en masse* measure up to this obligation and discharge it with fervor and effectiveness. This has not been the case on occasions in the past. When judges of our Fifth Circuit Court of Appeals, with courage and determination, faced the desegregation issue a few years ago, and governors and other public officials proudly displayed their contempt of court orders, there were lawyers—yes, lawyers—officers of the court—who were supporting this contemptuous conduct, some vociferously. It is a lawyer's duty not only to counsel a client against such contempts—it is the lawyer's obligation to denounce publicly all conduct that weakens the efficacy of the rule of law. And finally, it is the lawyer's high prerogative to lead his fellow citizens in honoring the law.

QUESTIONS AND ANSWERS

Leon Jaworski: I'm going to stop here at the close of the third lecture, and we'll pick up tomorrow morning on the fourth one. Now, we do have a full twenty minutes, even a little bit more than that, which I have deliberately allowed so that we can have ample time for the asking of questions and for giving me an opportunity to undertake to answer them. So, open for questioning now. Yes, sir.

Male Voice: Do you think that the use of juries makes the outcome so uncertain that sometimes it discourages or perhaps sometimes encourages settlements? The question I'm asking is, do you think juries encourage or discourage settlements?

Jaworski: That question is a very practical one and is one that lawyers face very often during trial of cases. And every lawyer tries to read a jury and tries to read them as they come back for more instructions; and tries to read them as the arguments are made; tries to even read them at the very beginning when the jury is being selected. And I can tell you they can misread them many times. It's very difficult—very difficult to determine whether a juror is for you or whether he's against you. The only instinct that I used at times was when the jury would come back in and either talk about having difficulty reaching a verdict or to ask for some more evidence to be read or to ask a question or tell the judge they'd like to go to dinner. Those that look at me from that jury box I thought might be in my favor and those who avoided looking at me I figured had no use for me and my side of the case. Now, this was not the most accurate yardstick to use. It was a little bit accurate to some degree, but all I'm saying to you is you really cannot read the jurors. Some will deliberately mislead you at times.

I'll never forget an experience that I had when I tried a case here in Waco. It was the second time the case was tried; it was a charge of double murder and a very, very horrible crime. It was tried, and I couldn't put him on the stand a second time because, truth of the matter is, he had confessed to me in between the first and second trials. We had obtained a new trial after his first conviction. And a juror came up to me just before we started the process of selecting a jury and he said, "Say, be sure and take me." I—I was a young lawyer. I had some grave doubts about this fellow. He spoke as if he meant business, you know, and so on, and I mentioned it to an older lawyer, told him about my doubts in taking this man. And the older lawyer said, "Well, I don't think you have much to lose; I think I'd go ahead and take him." And I did. And I want you to know that jury wasn't out very long and when they came in to bring in the death penalty, he led the parade. And he had in his hands the gun that was used; he had in his hands every bit of evidence, physical evidence, that had been introduced. And he was very proud to walk in there and return the death penalty. So from then on it wouldn't have done any juror any good to ever suggest to me that he be taken on a jury—it's a sure way of my scrapping him. You just never know. The art of selecting a jury is one that you learn in time. You might say, well, it condemns, in a sense, the jury system, but it doesn't do anything of the kind because somebody in the whole system, in the whole process, is still going to be a human being who's going to pass on this matter or a set of human beings, and I would just as soon trust those twelve I had never seen before, than I would someone whom I had known and seen over a period of time. Yes?

Male Voice: Do you feel that there's a need to go to a blue-chip jury for a complex antitrust matter or something like that?

Jaworski: Well, first let me tell you that I have an aversion to any kind of a blue-chip jury. Somehow or another, it just doesn't appeal to me. I think largely the experience that I've had with jurors after this period of time—and I will never try another jury case; that's over; my time has passed. But the experience that I've had with jurors is such as to cause me to be drawn to the rank-and-file selection of the jury. I strongly believe in it, and I've tried these cases in states other than Texas. I tried a case in California where women were on the jury and had not yet been permitted in Texas. It was rather a novel experience to me then. And I've learned to believe in my juries. I do realize, though, that in an antitrust case, you do have a real problem. I'm not sure, though, that the people who are supposed to have a high intellectual horizon are the best ones to select. They begin to substitute their ideas and their judgments for the evidence many times. I remember a case that we tried in Brazoria County, Texas, that had much technical evidence involved: the drilling of many oil wells; it involved, actually, the West Columbia oil field. And I was helping represent the Texas Company in the case and here was a jury composed of the rank and file of individuals that you would draw from a small country town, Angleton, Texas. I couldn't have been more impressed with how they followed the evidence and I would like to think understood it because it did return the right verdict. The point I'm making is that I think that, by and large, there's something to be said in favor of having a so-called blue-ribbon jury, but I don't want them myself. I will also say this, that the most difficulty I have seen with certain jurors is when they begin to think they know so much about something themselves that they begin to use their own ideas and their own opinions, rather than be controlled by the evidence of the case. And you're liable to run into that too often with so-called blue-ribbon juries. The next question, please. Yes.

Male Voice: Does the nature of the adversary system contribute to an impression among laymen that justice can be bought or purchased, in your opinion?

Jaworski: Certainly the adversary system does not find great favor with the laymen; many who have been in court, criticize it; those who win, praise it. But there are many who have observed trials, and they feel that there is a lot of lost motion going on and that there are endless objections by lawyers and so on. But its greatest asset is that it is a good way, if it is used properly, of ascertaining the truth. There's nothing like it—there you ask questions, under oath, until you have established the facts. And if you've done your job properly, the chances are, before the trial is over, the lawyers will have been able to get the truth from the witnesses. Many times the truth escapes them and many times it's due to inadequate preparation on the part of lawyers. Today, I think it's wholly inexcusable for a lawyer not to be fully prepared at the time of the trial and not to know what the facts are, because there are endless—as Professor Matt Dawson has explained to you, and will explain to you—endless opportunities for the taking of depositions and obtaining evidence in advance, to know pretty well what the facts are at the time of trial. I think it takes the sport out of the trial to a large degree but, we just can't help that; we're still seeking justice. I think that, today, with all the advancements that have been made in pre-trial discovery, I think that the jousting, the sport of combat, in the courtroom, has been lessened to some degree. But we should not mourn that; we should praise that, really. All right. Yes, sir.

Male Voice: Would you comment on the impact of the high cost of litigation with regard to access to the equal justice concept of law?

Jaworski: Well, it's just a deplorable situation, and I don't know at the moment what the answer is to it, but an answer has to be found. And it's being studied now; the large bar associations, like the Association of the Bar of the City of New York, are studying it; the American Bar Association is studying it, of course, and every effort is being made to find an answer to it. I don't know what the answer to it is going to be. Here is the simple fact, that you cannot begin a lawsuit now and do a good job of it, for a client, that is, take your deposition, your interrogatories, go through your pre-trial proceedings—unless that client has a pretty good war-chest to support all of the cost of that. Expert witnesses—gee—they're almost out of reach in what they expect by way of their per diem and their cost of preparation. And all of that is a very, very disquieting factor. When it really gets down to it, it is a question of how much can an individual put into the trial of the lawsuit? How much money is available? Now, in some of the plaintiff's cases, some of the damage suits, the lawyers, to a degree, support that. They believe in that case; they have it on a contingent fee arrangement and they support it by putting out the money themselves. But, think of the many other cases—and what disturbs me especially is the plight of the so-called white-collar worker—and I don't want to exclude the blue-collar worker from this situation either, but it applies, perhaps, a little bit more to the white-collar worker, who has an income—let's say, just for sake of illustration—of twenty to twenty-five thousand dollars a year; he has a family to support; he has a good lawsuit or a good defense to a case that has been filed against him. Now how is he going to employ lawyers and find the money for litigation—the cost of litigation, with that sort of an income? He has a family to support. Now, we have to absolutely find an answer to that; there just has to be found an answer to it or else this talk of equal justice under the law is completely lost. I think this is the most dangerous situation facing our society, as far as our system of justice is concerned. Today, the man who has no means—as we will discuss a little bit more in depth later on—does have a way of getting lawyers to represent him because of the support that is being given to those who are poverty-stricken and the representation of their rights. But that's not true of the man who can't qualify as a pauper, so to speak. All right. Yes.

Male Voice: Do you think the adversary system is threatened by the growth of administrative law?

Jaworski: Yes, I certainly do. And it's threatened by what I think will be future growth. I think that administrative law will come into play more and more; and as was noted yesterday, more and more efforts at arbitration will necessarily follow. But there is a strong—a very strong leaning toward administrative law and to the expansion of administrative law on the part of many. They feel that it's partly the answer to what our problem is today. Okay, do we have other questions? Yes, sir.

Male Voice: Having seen both systems at work, do you feel that our state district judges should be given more power to structure the proceedings and participate in them, such as federal judges have?

Jaworski: Ahhhh, that's a very, very difficult one to answer. You see, you almost have to say it depends on the judge, which is a very, very poor answer—which is no answer at all. Again, as far as determining the facts, as far as being the trier of facts, I still want my jurors. I don't want just that judge. Now, there are certain things that perhaps the judge should be able to do and he may be given some of that authority in time, that he doesn't have now, that would expedite a trial. There's always a very strong clash among lawyers and the viewing of the matter of whether such practices, such procedure should be streamlined. Usually, you'll find many of the defendants' lawyers who oppose it. They feel that some of their weapons are taken away from them. Plaintiffs' lawyers will laugh at it, because plaintiff's lawyers are just interested in getting the matter before a jury, you know, and especially if they have a case that looks like they're going to get a good basketful of damages. They are all interested in just cutting through everything; getting the facts before the jury and there it is. Now, I think that probably our judges have been given, by and large, in this state, the authority that seems to be expedient, unless we're going to change the system some. And I don't advocate that. There are constantly improvements, as you will learn through your courses and probably have learned already, that show the new changes, the new direction in which some of our procedural tactics now go. But it's a far cry from when I first began trying lawsuits. As a matter of fact, it became for a while much more difficult, when the special issue system went into effect, which was not used at the time when I first started my cases. It came into effect about that time. The special issue era caused a tremendous change in the trial of lawsuits. And as a consequence, there were many errors committed; there were many reversals. And defendants' lawyers, especially in negligence cases, strongly believed in the special issue system, because they didn't want the jury to know who was winning the lawsuit and that theoretically was the reason for adopting the special issue instead of the general charge instruction. As you know, the system changes from state to state. You don't have the same system here that you do elsewhere. And in the federal court, you have, right now, about all that is needed in order to have a very simple, direct method of submitting a case to a jury. You do not have the same problems, the same hurdles, and the same barriers as you do in state court. We have time for another question, I believe, Dean, and then—I think we adjourn. I'll take one more question.

Male Voice: You noted in your lecture that you didn't feel that the adversary system could handle such items as the censorship of movies and literature and the prosecution of victimless crimes. I wondered if you were suggesting, perhaps, the adoption of Justice Douglas' feelings in this regard and if not, what are you suggesting?

Jaworski: What I was suggesting is that we need to devote effort, study and attention to how to make the adversary system simpler than it is at the present time—to cut out just as much of those matters that can be fairly and properly eliminated and get to the issue; saying that if we didn't do it that I have the fear that we will be turning to other efforts and that we will find ourselves confronted with the use of devices other than that system for the purpose of settling disputes. Now, you said something about Mr. Justice Douglas. What did you say about him?

Male Voice: Well, I was wondering if—especially in regard to the censorship of any movies, periodicals and whatnot, he had rather a strong stance in that regard—that the system—our system of justice had no place and that it was unconstitutional. And I wondered whether you were saying that the adversary system should not be involved in it at all—

Jaworski: Oh, no. No, I think the adversary system, to some degree, has been the saving grace about some of the matters that might otherwise have come to pass. I'm a strong believer in the adversary system, and I would hate to see its influence impaired or lessened at all. I hope it stays strong. But I'm pointing out the dangers that might weaken it. I'm talking about things that get to be issues where the public takes a very strong stand; where finally there is a loss of confidence in the system, and that's when substitutes are offered. And that is when we begin to run in all directions—sociological solutions and everything else—and this is what I'm warning about.

Well, my time is up, Dean. And let me just say to you, I look forward to being with you tomorrow morning. Thank you.

IV

The Practice of Law

Because I began the practice of law at a rather young age, I have seen the profession firsthand over a fifty-five year period. The transitions that have taken place since then are marked and considerable, so much so that the practice of law today bears no reasonable resemblance to what it was in 1925.

A. *Progression Toward Specialization*

Perhaps it would be helpful, to illustrate my point, to describe the different types of legal matters that I would undertake to handle from day to day when I first began the practice of law in Waco. I would do both office work and trial work. I handled both civil matters and criminal matters. On a given day it would not be at all unusual for me to be preparing a deed of conveyance in the morning and to be in what we called city court—termed today commonly as municipal court—to defend a vagrant or some other misdemeanant. The next day I could very well be preparing a will and spending the rest of the day in preparation of the defense of a burglary case in the state criminal district court. I had a fair clientele of bootleggers so it was not unusual, whenever the United States District Court was sitting in Waco, for me to be over there representing one charged with the violation of the Volstead Act under the 18th Amendment. I handled this latter type of case as far away as Laredo in the south and El Paso in the west. The work I disliked the most was that of examining abstracts of title—something that is now an art of the past inasmuch as title companies have taken over this work. To sit there for several hours and turn page after page of a thick abstract to determine whether the claimed owner had good and marketable title to convey was the object. The writing of the opinion was always a bore to me—but it had to be done because it was part of the practice. Divorce cases were much fewer in those days, but now and then I even ran into one of those. Back at that time the title to land was not always settled by any means, and there were a certain number of trespass to try title cases that needed to be disposed of in order to clear title satisfactorily. Some of these were contested. At times the claimant rested his title on adverse possession. I even tried that type of case after I moved to Houston. Perhaps one of the most bitter and hotly fought cases which I tried involved a trespass to try title case in which a doctor, of all people, was claiming that he held some very valuable land in Galveston County by having fenced the property for ten years and held it openly and notoriously adversely to the record owner. There were no income tax cases or problems, in fact no tax cases of any kind unless they related to ad valorem cases. There was no securities law and no labor law, and unless you represented a bank there was very little to learn about banking law.

Some lawyers did concentrate on the trial of criminal cases and undertook only a smattering of civil work. They were known as criminal lawyers and were employed at times by civil lawyers to assist them, and usually were the lawyers to whom the average criminal case went for employment.

Now and then a lawyer was looked upon as a specialist, but this was primarily in the field of criminal law. Otherwise, a lawyer was just a practitioner and would be prepared to take on whatever matter came to him. The law firms in Waco were small, and this was true even of the larger firms in the state. The largest firms were in Houston and Dallas, but even they would be considered quite small by today's standards.

The day of specialization came along in later years, and when it did begin it moved along very swiftly. We know that there occurred a fast evolution of administrative law in Washington and also to some degree at the state level, and this required the work of what we term office lawyers who became specialists in this type of work. Today the general practitioner is an item of the past. There is no lawyer who can serve properly a client whose business is widespread and not require the assistance of specialists in the various fields that pertain to the client's overall legal requirements.

If I may use the setup in our law firm as an illustration of the present state of affairs—we presently are divided into sections. There are partners and associates assigned to each section, in addition to paralegals. The firm which had ten lawyers when I joined it now has 280. The sections include admiralty, corporation, banking and business, energy, family law, international law, labor, litigation, oil, gas and utilities, patents, public law, real estate, tax, transportation and trust and estates.

Speaking of specialization, a friend of mine practicing in the valley of this state was approached by a prospective client who was charged with a crime in the county where my friend was practicing law. The prospective client told him of his problems and explained to him that he had no witnesses. He detailed the witnesses who were opposing him and explained that all of them were well known in the county and highly regarded. He also explained that he had been convicted of a crime before and had served time in the penitentiary. He further remarked that the judge before whom the case was pending regarded him as an unworthy individual. With that he paused and looked at the lawyer and asked, "Do you take a case of that kind?" The lawyer paused a moment and then said, "Yes, but I do not like to specialize in them."

A good indication of the vicissitudes of the law practice can be gained from a look at the curriculum of the law student in my day and that which you face in law school today. There are numerous additions, and these have been brought about by the complications in our societal life as well as in the metamorphosis of business undertakings. It has also been brought about by increasing government intrusion in the affairs of the citizen.

Given the metamorphosis that has taken place during the half century past, one might conclude that the day of change has come to an end and that matters nowadays would continue on a somewhat stationary basis. This is a false assumption. The truth is that the legal profession has more innovations and complexities facing it now than at any time in its history. This does not mean that the profession was asleep during that period of time and did nothing to come to grips with the challenges that it faced. It does mean that no sooner was one problem met or at least reasonably contained, than another came to add to the overall burdens.

In my day as a fledgling lawyer and for quite sometime thereafter, I never heard of a seminar or any type of conference or meeting for the purpose of improving the ability of the lawyer. Legal education was confined to the law schools and to the lawyers' offices and by the trial and error method in the courtroom. There was no State Bar of Texas course on continuing legal education—there was no Southwestern Legal Foundation or other type of institution that brought lawyers together for instruction and learning in special phases of the law.

There were some giants at the Bar, and many of these had obtained their education through study in someone's law office. Some of the more outstanding lawyers of the state practiced in smaller communities. A city lawyer going to a rural community to try a lawsuit usually had his hands full regardless of how good a case he had. The local lawyer in a rural community was looked upon as an oracle, and the good people of that township usually went to him for advice not only on legal matters

41

but on all of their other problems as well—except perhaps medical or spiritual. So not only were these small town lawyers quite skilled in the art of advocacy—they also had the respect and esteem of their fellow-townsmen. As a consequence, the city lawyer facing the home-town advocate was at a distinct disadvantage. City lawyers who had a case in a smaller community soon learned to employ local counsel to offset their home-town adversary. The local counsel would assist in the selection of a jury and usually make at least one of the jury arguments.

There were no elaborate codes of ethics and codes of responsibility in existence in those days, but by and large lawyers lived up to a certain code of conduct—especially in dealing with one another. I do not recall any grievance committees' actions. I do recall that after I moved to Houston I was a counsel on behalf of the State Bar of Texas in disbarring a lawyer who had misappropriated some of his client's funds. There was some "ambulance-chasing" on the part of a few lawyers. This was not a frequent occurrence, and when it happened it was rather crudely done. Nowadays there is a much more widespread practice of what is termed "ambulance-chasing," but it is done in a more refined manner than in my early years.

We know that in current times almost every issue of the *Texas Bar Journal* records a number of disciplinary actions, including disbarment. In some instances these are voluntary cancellations of licenses to avoid disciplinary action.

B. *Advocacy in the Practice of Law*

I do wish to spend some of my time in discussing with you advocacy—perhaps I should say "adequate advocacy." I will not discuss one of my favorite subjects with you, namely the *art* of advocacy, as you will learn that from your eminent professor, Matt Dawson. The particulars in writing briefs and in the handling of appellate arguments you will learn in your moot court program.

All of you undoubtedly have read in the last two years of the movement spearheaded by Chief Justice Burger to improve trial advocacy. I consider the Chief Justice quite well qualified to speak on this subject, from personal knowledge, on the arguments he hears before the United States Supreme Court. Though I am convinced that his whole purpose is to be objective and constructive, I am not certain that all of his statistics are correct as concerns the work of the advocate at the trial level. It is true that a few other federal judges, especially at the appellate level, have made some comments similar to that of the Chief Justice's, but obviously most of their information must come from other sources and not as a result of personally hearing and observing advocacy at the trial level in state and federal courts.

Let me begin these observations by saying that in my judgment the trial bar in this state is not composed of the outstanding and magnetic trial lawyers that I saw at work in 1930 to 1950. Undoubtedly this is true in large measure because the trial of cases has become so much more procedurally complicated in the latter period. In my early years, the trial lawyer was usually an excellent performer in the courtroom. He was alert, sharp, articulate, a good actor and a good orator. Except in some criminal cases, he did not bother too much with the niceties of a court's charge. Charging a jury was much less complicated in those days. He was usually a very forceful character in the courtroom keeping a jury spellbound by his questioning of witnesses, his arguments to the court and, of course, by the final summations to the jury. But this alone was not enough to make him effective. He also had to be well versed in the law. All of the trial stratagems and tactics an advocate can employ in the courtroom could be shattered by just one adverse holding of the higher court on a point of law.

I recall when I was still in Waco I had a matter before the county judge. I was without any legal precedent to support my position, so I undertook to gain the court's attention and seek sympathy by engaging in a fervent appeal to his emotions. When I finished, an eminent trial lawyer at the Waco bar who knew me quite well came up and simply said, "You know, Leon, you could have saved yourself those many minutes of effort if you had had just one case in point to support your position. You could have cited it in one minute and then sat down." He was right, and his comment made quite an impression on me. Even as far back as the 17th Century an English lawyer named Sir Matthew Hale, who was considered to have had a great mastery of the common law, opined, "If the judge or jury has a right understanding, oratory signifies nothing but a waste of time and lots of words."

For many years there were young lawyers who, upon graduation from law school, were ill-equipped to enter the courtroom. This was not true of Baylor graduates, but it was true of graduates from even such outstanding law schools as the University of Texas. I well recall how Judge Norman Atkinson who presided over the Eleventh Judicial District Court of Harris County in Houston once told me that he could always spot a Baylor graduate when a young lawyer came into his court. He said that invariably the Baylor graduate would know his way around and seemed to be at home. Other young lawyers who had their schooling at other law schools, he said, showed a complete ignorance of what it was all about—even in dealing with the clerk of the court.

I will invade Professor Dawson's domain just long enough to tell you that I believe one of the greatest assets to a young (and old) trial lawyer is to have an understanding of just the most ordinary basics of psychology—that of understanding human nature and especially knowing something of how to deal with other human beings. The entire process in the courtroom is administered by humans—by the judge—by the witnesses—by opposing counsel—by the jurors—even by the clerk, the court reporter and the bailiff. From the time that the selection of the jury begins, there is a constant opportunity for the lawyer to call on the use of principles of psychology, and how well he applies them may go far in determining the outcome of the case. You may well say that law suits should not be controlled by such factors. But there is no way to keep human instincts and traits from playing a part in the judicial process.

As far back as February, 1972 when I had the honor of serving as president of the American Bar Association, I commented on the President's Page of the *American Bar Journal* on the problem of courtroom advocacy. This is in part what I said at that time:

> The view that courtroom advocacy is a declining art is widely held among lawyers. That opinion comes out, often with more than a touch of sadness, in conversations among practitioners. Accomplished trial lawyers are in short supply at a time when the number of lawyers and the volume of litigation are soaring.
>
> Something now is being done about that paradox. This summer at the University of Colorado in Boulder the National Institute for Trial Advocacy will offer its first advanced training course in trial practice for approximately one hundred lawyers.
>
> The establishment of the institute is an important step forward in professional education. It will help stimulate in the American trial Bar a new emphasis on the importance of advocacy and a quest for forensic excellence in trial practice, which long have been looked upon as hallmarks of the British Bar. In these ways the institute will help enhance the stature of the profession and the quality of its services to clients in the years ahead.

Although I know of none as deeply rooted and as well conducted as Baylor Law School's courses on trial advocacy, the advent of such courses in other schools throughout the land, in the last decade particularly, has been most noticeable and heartening. There is hardly a law school of stature today that does not place some emphasis on advocacy in its curriculum.

Some appellate courts, due to their case loads—and this is true particularly in some of the U. S. Circuit Courts of Appeals—have undertaken to eliminate oral argument in some cases and in others to limit the time to a shorter period. This has been resisted by groups of trial lawyers in the belief that it would hamper the proper presentation of issues involved in their appeals. Certainly the enlarged case loads of some courts need to be reckoned with, but I agree that it would be unfortunate to restrain oral

advocacy to the point of being inadequate or insufficient due to lack of
time. It has been my experience that where undetermined points of law
are involved, as is true in so many cases on appeal, the courts need the
full benefit of an oral presentation and have been greatly helped by a
thorough ventilating of the points of law involved. In cases where the
appeal is frivolous and involves no more than points of law already
settled, one would agree that oral argument is superfluous.

QUESTIONS AND ANSWERS

Leon Jaworski: —I discussed with Dean McSwain one matter this
morning that had not been mentioned to you by me, and he approves of
it. You may have some Watergate questions, and I don't want you to be
reticent about asking these so long as they do have a legal aspect. If they
relate to any phase of what occurred and the handling of these matters as
to the proceedings in court, as to the reasons why we did this, chose this
avenue or did this particular thing instead of the other—this is all quite
pertinent and it's perfectly all right for you to ask these questions. Now,
we cannot discuss Watergate at length in these sessions; it's absolutely
impossible to do that. But any such questions as you have that are of
particular interest to you, the Dean tells me he's agreeable that they are
within bounds. So we'll open the session to questions.

Male Voice: Mr. Jaworski, as a personal matter, if you had graduated
from Baylor law school in 1980, do you think you would hang out your
shingle in a small town or go to Houston with Fulbright and Jaworski?

Jaworski: Well, I think that's a very good question. Before it's all over
with we're going to talk some about that. This is one of the parts of the
lectures that is to come. I would just say this to you, that I think it all
depends upon the style of your life. I had started here and then I went to
Houston because I had an opportunity to go, not to a large law firm at
first, but to a small organization. And then I had a chance to go with this
present firm of mine. I wistfully look at the experiences that I had when
I was not in a large organization. But I must also say to you that there is
something about a large organization and going through the chairs, so
to speak, in that organization and then sitting where you eventually do,
that also is quite gratifying. There are certain things that you lose by
going to a large firm, a large organization; there are certain things that
you gain by going. Now, it depends very much on the individual. In
today's situation it wouldn't take very much for me to kiss mine good-
bye and go to a small one, you know. And the factors, the whole
situation has changed. I say that in jest to some degree but also say that

there's nothing that I think is more wonderful than to be practicing in a small community where you have an opportunity to talk to people about everything that comes along in that community. All right. I'll tell you someone who can tell you more about that, even though his community was not too small, but Matt Dawson practiced in Corsicana for a number of years and by comparison with cities such as Houston, it is a small community. And I think he can tell you the difference in the situation. Now, I had a question back yonder. Yes, sir?

Male Voice: You spoke briefly about trial attorneys and that particular area of practice. Do you feel that's one of the areas that needs the most improvement?

Jaworski: Well, I don't share the view that the trial bar is as bad as Chief Justice Burger and some others say. Early in the lectures, you remember I said to you that I believe it's a matter of preparation more than the ability of the individual lawyer. I told you that I had seen some lawyers who had greater talents but who performed rather poorly in court because they just didn't prepare themselves thoroughly. And then I'd seen some who had no great talent but who really worked at it, prepared themselves, and did a very commendable job in the courtroom. I think that, although I pointed out to you that I don't see the magnetic talent in the courtroom these days, there are very good trial lawyers. And I think that the manner of the training that one receives at this law school, for example, plus the readiness to apply yourself, to work hard at it, to thoroughly prepare your cases—I don't see a reason on earth why any individual who's had the benefit of the courses here and then works at it—I see no reason why that individual shouldn't become a good trial lawyer. And in order to be a good and effective trial lawyer, you don't have to be looked upon as a sensational or as a brilliant sort of an individual. In civil trials of civil cases, I must say to you that there are a number of very, very fine trial lawyers. The number that are admitted to the American College of Trial Lawyers each year from Texas speaks for itself, and there are ever so many more who are nominated and who would like to get in and who do not make the list. The reason they don't is because there are just some who are better. All right, we'll take the next question. Yes, sir?

Male Voice: Mr. Jaworski, do you feel that it would be beneficial to have in our legal educational system some sort of mandatory clinical experience, like say, you know, an internship in the medical profession?

Jaworski: Well, now, that's a good question. I don't know whether all of you heard it; it's a question that relates to whether it should be required that a lawyer have a certain amount of clinical experience— actual experience—as a part of the training, somewhat similar to what is required when a person becomes a doctor. A certain amount of good

46

experience, we all know, is required and must be had before he receives his license to practice.

Well, some of that clinical experience can be received in various ways. It's not open to everybody unfortunately, because they don't know that there are enough places to go around. As you know, there are many who serve as law clerks after they have been in school for two years. There are many firms who actually seek these students and want them to come in and spend some time, the advantage being that they have an opportunity to look the firms over, learn something about the practice, and decide maybe which particular specialty they would like to follow. They get this clinical experience and also give the law firm or the lawyer, whoever it may be, an opportunity to size up this individual or these individuals for the purpose of seeing whether they should be given an opportunity to join that organization. The work that these men and women, who have been in law school and finished two years, perform in our law firm, for instance, absolutely amazes me. It just seems incredible how much progress they've made in two years and how much help they can be already, just working there as clerks during that summer. Now, that is the kind of clinical experience, of course, you're talking about, but it's not open to everyone because there are just not enough places to go around. And a requirement, of course, that you have, the individual have, some clinical experience, I think is very important. Trial of cases—you get it now, because you have an actual, ongoing advocacy program here we used to call practice court. But you don't perhaps get the clinical experience in other respects. Some of you may have an opportunity to work in some of the Waco firms at times—law firms—and have an opportunity to see what goes on. All I can say to you is that some of that is just absolutely invaluable because sooner or later you're going to have to pick it up, and you don't want to pick it up at the expense of your clients when you've got your law practice. If you don't get it sooner, that's just the way it's liable to work out. So, it is something that I think that the profession should address itself to, working together with the law school, to see that the maximum of openings are available to the law students, certainly beginning at the end of two years, if not sooner. Now, there are in many places, as you know, where law schools and law students may work in the morning—I mean, have their classes in the morning and work in the afternoon. If you'll pardon it, I had alluded to this before, but this is what I did. I worked. I attended classes in the morning and worked in the afternoons as a stenographer in a law office. In Washington, when I was working on my Master's, I worked on the Hill in the afternoon, and those experiences were of tremendous value to me.

V

The Organized Bar

I should like to devote a few minutes to comments on the organized bar, both on the state and national level. This is a very important, and I believe indispensible, part of the profession and without a functional, organized bar, the profession is bound to suffer and eventually deteriorate.

A. *The Texas Bar*

In Texas, where we have an integrated bar, every lawyer belongs to the State Bar of Texas. The last legislature undertook to tamper with the status of our bar and for quite some time it was undetermined whether, in fact, we would have an integrated bar. Some of the opposition to our present status came from sources who objected to the payment of dues; still others objected to the assessments to help pay for the remaining indebtedness on the State Bar Center in Austin—one of the finest and most useful in the country. Some of the efforts to weaken the Bar came from legislators and other who were venting their spleen because of personal animosities. Undoubtedly, some who sought changes in the status of the bar thought such moves would be constructive, but personally I found little or no value in their arguments. This is not to say that the State Bar of Texas has not made its mistakes—so have all organizations of that type at one time or another.

A number of those favoring a change in our present structure desired to have the operations of the State Bar subject to fiscal appropriations granted by the legislature. This was wholly unacceptable to me and to others who had long been interested in the operations of our State Bar. If the Bar were to be dependent upon legislative appropriations, it would lose its independence. Even more so, with so many lawyers being members of the legislature, such control would soon involve conflicts of interest and undoubtedly result in self-serving actions harmful to the public interest. Although the State Bar finally gained a continuance of

49

its existence during the last legislative session, it had to make some concessions including that of having representatives of the laity serve on the Bar's Board of Directors and on its grievance committees. One could not quarrel with efforts to improve the work of some of our grievance committees, but I am not at all certain that the changes made are of substantial assistance. Such assaults on our profession's status in this state would never have been undertaken ten years ago, much less succeed. Our profession's clout had weakened and our detractors took advantage of this.

B. *The American Bar*

The national spokesman of the profession is the American Bar Association—its only spokesman on matters of uniform significance to the Bar. There are other organizations of lawyers, but none has the national recognition enjoyed by the American Bar Association. I consider its viable existence so important to the profession that I want to devote a few minutes in discussing it with you.

I admit to a strong sense of partisanship in discussing the American Bar Association. It is impossible for me to separate myself from the personally gratifying experiences I enjoyed during my year of its presidency from 1972-1973. I do want to be objective in presenting the organization to you, and in order to be free of possible bias in my comments, I have selected an excerpt from Erwin Griswold's book, *Law and Lawyers in the United States.* Griswold was Dean of Harvard Law School for a number of years and later served as Solicitor General of the United States. Here are his comments:

> The American Bar Association, our first National organization of lawyers, was organized at Saratoga Springs, New York in 1878. At first, and for many years, its objectives were chiefly social, and it was a rather exclusive organization, open only to those who were regarded as leaders of the bar in their communities.
>
> After 25 years, in 1903, the American Bar Association had 2,000 members. Ten years later, in 1913, it had 8,000 members. In 1928, after 50 years, it had 28,000 members. In 1950 its membership was 42,000. Not long after that, it ceased to be especially exclusive and sought memberships from lawyers throughout the country. This has resulted in a great increase in membership, so that the Association now has 115,000 members, which is close to half of all of the active lawyers in the country.
>
> But the American Bar Association remains a volunteer organization; and though it has considerable influence in many fields, it has no real powers over any member of the profession. The most that it can do in the way of discipline is to suspend or expel a member, but this does not affect his right to practice law. The Association's

Canons of Ethics are widely looked to and have been adopted in many of the States. And the opinions of its Committee on Ethics have great influence.

In 1936, the structure of the Association was completely reorganized. At that time, final power to speak for the Association was placed in a House of Delegates, which now numbers about 300 members. One of these from each State is elected by a mail ballot of the Association members in that State, for a three year term. He is known as the State Delegate. Then there are members representing State and local bar associations, the various Sections of the American Bar Association, certain affiliated associations, and some public officers, such as the Attorney General and the Solicitor General of the United States. The House of Delegates ordinarily meets twice a year, for three or four days at a time. Its deliberations and consideration are usually on a high level, and in recent years especially there has been a marked tendency to consider matters from a broad point of view not unduly influenced by the interests of clients.

Apart from the main body of the American Bar Association, its members have the opportunity of belonging to any one or more of its many Sections. These deal with such matters as Labor Law, Administrative Law, Real Property, Probate and Trust Law, Tax Law, Antitrust Law, and Business or Corporate Law. Much of the most effective work of the Association is done in these Sections. It is the one great National organization of lawyers in our country. We are a profession, and we are more likely to become an effective profession if we work together on our common professional problems.

The American Bar Association is now engaged in what is termed its Second Century Fund campaign. The overall purpose of this undertaking is not only to make the Association members aware of the responsibilities that are ours but as well to undergird the Association financially so that it can continue its work in the future. Some of the financial assistance the Association received on through the years had dried up and some of it fell into question under a ruling of the Internal Revenue Service. As a consequence, the Association had to look to new sources for additional funds and this primarily prompted The Second Century Fund Campaign, which I am privileged to serve as chairman.

To give you a bird's eye view of the status of the Association and its look to the future, I will restate some of the comments that I made at the General Assembly of the American Bar Association Annual Meeting on August 13 of last year. At that time I stated:

> I am not here to speak on public issues or events, not even to comment on any of the programs now conducted by our Association on behalf of our society. I am here to speak self-servingly—selfishly, if you please. Self-serving in the sense of preserving a profession in which I take great pride. More importantly, self-serving in the sense

51

of enabling our profession to continue to serve our society in leadership capacities, which has been its special prerogative.

Fifty-four years ago, on an occasion similar to this, one of the great men of our profession and of our country, Charles Evans Hughes, spoke to the national leaders of the bar of that era. His address was titled "Liberty and Law", and it included a statement of such prescience, and such relevance to what I will be saying here today, that I quote it now. These words of Chief Justice Hughes delivered as president of this Association in 1925: *"Let us rise to our opportunity* as guardians of the traditions which constitute the precious possession of our democracy, *and play our part in establishing and making secure the authority of law as the servant of liberty wisely conceived. . . ."*

He was speaking at the halfway point in the Association's First Century. We were, of course, much fewer in number then, less well organized, less publicly active as a profession, and no doubt less able to foresee the extent and urgency of the challenges that confront us now.

Even so, Hughes perceived clearly the perils that lay ahead were we to shirk our professional responsibilities. And he did not hesitate to sound the warning that if the Bar failed to respond adequately to public needs, if it did abrogate its leadership role in the public affairs, we could expect to see its authority to govern itself challenged by powerful critics in and out of government. It was a wise warning then, and it still is.

Were Chief Justice Hughes with us today, he might well be standing here offering the same admonition. Only one word, I believe, would be changed. The condition of the world today—and the enormously increased prestige and structure of this Association— no longer allow us to speak of rising to our *opportunity*. We have known for sometime that we no longer have the luxury of viewing our role as a mere *opportunity*, to be seized or not as we choose. Today, we can speak only of rising to our *responsibilities*. There is no other word for it. There is no other choice.

There are constant pressures upon our profession—from within our own ranks and from the government and the public at large—to respond to a multitude of complex and difficult challenges.

In the face of such challenges, the imperatives of professionalism are cast in new dimensions. For the American Bar Association, the imperative is one of professional leadership. We cannot expect state and local bar associations, however strong and influential they may be, to assume that responsibility on a national level. The organized bar cannot hope to meet the enormous challenges we face unless this Association—the preeminent professional organization of lawyers in America—is prepared to provide the bold and effective leadership that all great endeavors require. And to ensure that we are prepared, we must marshall our resources—both human and financial—and we must do so without delay.

Hughes, Root and other giants of our profession and leaders of this Association, as well as their colleagues, bequeathed to us the glories and traditions of a proud profession, nobly regarded for its illustrious contributions to our free society. This rich legacy was entrusted to us not to dissipate but to preserve, and, as our members increase, to strengthen and enlarge. So I put this simple but direct question to you—even as I put it to myself. Are we going faithfully to embrace this sacred trust and jealously preserve it for this and future generations of America? You and I will provide the answer.

And a year later I was privileged again to stand before the General Assembly of the American Bar Association and announce that we had reached a $3 million mark in pledges. Individual lawyers and law firms across the land were sending in their contributions. The campaign was then—and is now—going extremely well, causing me to say that the legal profession was giving a resounding answer to the cynics who question whether we—the lawyers—really care about our future.

C. *Ethical Responsibilities*

Before I close this particular series of my lectures, I would like to say a few words about ethical considerations as an integral part of our profession. In my view, once we lower the ethical barrier and proceed without regard to the fundamental rules the profession has generally observed, the profession will lose its lustre and become commercialistic from core to core.

For years I have embraced the words of an Irish judge in the cause of The Queen vs. O'Connell. His name is Mr. Justice Crampton, and he spoke in 1844. Here are his words on the ethics of the advocate:

> If he be the advocate of an individual, and retained and remunerated (often inadequately) for his valuable services, yet he has a prior and perpetual retainer on behalf of truth and justice; and there is no Crown or other license which in any case or for any party or purpose can discharge him from that primary and paramount retainer.

The whole point is simply this: if we want to be considered as members of a profession, we have to demean ourselves as such. We cannot claim the advantages inherent in professional status and at the same time fail to keep our own house in order, thereby permitting our affairs to drift into unethical demeanor—even if only on the part of a small percentage of the membership. I might add that if we are to ape the secondhand car dealer with advertisements of one kind and another and conduct our business in the basement of merchandise shops, we are suggesting to the public that we are no more than any other over-the-counter business venture and deserve to be treated as such.

Sometime ago I read that young people were turning to law schools because the practice of law was offering better opportunities than other professions. The article spoke of young men and women having had in mind becoming engineers and finding that there was an overcrowded condition in the engineering profession and that young graduates faced difficulties in obtaining employment. About that time I knew of some young college graduates who had changed their intended careers by turning to the study of law because of the financial opportunities it offered.

Why are you studying law? Is it solely because you look upon it as a promising means to an end—the end being a good livelihood? If finances are to be the only reward under consideration, then I seriously doubt that you will be enjoying the practice of law. More so, you will be losing some of its greatest rewards—especially the reward of having offered helpful service to your fellowman in the preservation of his rights and liberties. Personally, I know of no greater thrill, no deeper satisfaction than to realize at the end of a long struggle in the courtroom, for example, that someone's liberty has been preserved or that someone's rights have been protected.

I am concerned about the lawyer who does no more in life by way of contributing to society than to show up at his office each morning and leave in the evening with his whole time having been devoted solely to the practice of law and with no regard having been indicated for, and no effort undertaken to join in, the endeavors that have as their goal the improvement of our society and the solution of the problems it faces.

There are periods in a lawyer's struggle for survival when there is little time for extracurricular activities. But there comes a time when he can do both, and he should never shirk the latter. The lawyer is gifted with an understanding and with experience that enables him to be of great assistance in the meeting of community problems of one kind and another. For him or her to abstain in the use of these talents is inexcusable and gives support to the cynical contention of some that lawyers are merely interested in fees and nothing else.

A busy trial practice which requires labors not only in the courtroom during the day but in the office by way of preparation for the following day often precludes active participation in anything else. But the time comes when there is opportunity for other service. I went through this cycle myself, and all I can say is that such opportunities do come in time, and when they come they should not be neglected.

You may be asking for an illustration. If so, I have one—a program in which every lawyer can and should participate regardless of his specialty—regardless of whether he is practicing in a small community or a large city. It relates to the establishment in the elementary and high schools of an improved program of training in the responsibilities of citizenship.

Clearly evident in 1960 was the neglect of which we had been guilty in the area of youth education in citizenship respects. We had experienced what can only be described as a breakdown in the teaching of the root principles of law in a free society. We had failed to make clear to the very young how the law functions to protect individual rights and provides for orderly, democratic change; the difference between dissent and violent protest; the necessity to balance civil rights with civic responsibility. The blame for that breakdown rested not alone with the schools but with the home, the church, and the community, and to a considerable extent with the legal profession itself.

In Dallas, Texas, for example, such a program has been conducted for a number of years. Lawyers not only assist in setting up the program in schools, but assist teachers in their training and make themselves available to answer particular questions students or teachers may raise from time to time. The program has brought great results. Today's youth are more aware of the need of having rules of conduct in the preservation of our society and are more receptive to such instruction than ever before. It is our obligation to keep them informed so that there will not be recurrences of some of the ugly experiences in the 1960s.

QUESTIONS AND ANSWERS

Leon Jaworski: So now, Dean McSwain, with your permission we will go into the question and answer period. I am allowing enough time for us to not be cut short. I realize that to some degree undertaking to answer your questions in this particular period is more important than what I may be saying to you in this lecture. The contents of the lecture may be something that you already are aware of or something you already have in mind, but there may be some questions that you have that you feel additional light should be cast upon. And if I can do so, I want to. So let me hear from you.

Male Voice: Mr. Jaworski, according to a recent survey, sixty percent of Americans had never used an attorney for any purpose and the reasons were that, first, they couldn't afford one and secondly, even if they could afford one, they didn't know how to find a good attorney. My question is this: what do you see as one's professional responsibility to counter this mind set and to provide accessibility to legal services for all the public?

Jaworski: Well, I think that you trust and know and agree that this is the greatest of all concerns of the American Bar Association and the profession as a whole at the present time. How does one go about selecting a lawyer? How do you know that you have a lawyer who is really able to perform? The lawyer has the right to hang his shingle on the outside of his office, and it says attorney-at-law and that's as much as the average person knows. Some people have never had the occasion to use a lawyer before they need a lawyer. Now, they walk into this particular lawyer's office, and they place the matter before him. In today's complicated and complex situations in the practice of law, that lawyer may be competent to advise that client—to help in that situation—and then again, he may not. It's a clear duty of the lawyer in that situation to make certain that the client gets in the hands of a lawyer who is thoroughly competent and qualified to handle that particular matter. Now, often that is not done. The lawyer will attempt to handle it and you cannot blame the client. The client walks in, in effect blind-folded and totally ignorant, and there is no way the client can pass upon the qualifications of that lawyer. Sometimes they make inquiry and somebody says, well, lawyer so-and-so is pretty well known, you know, and they've heard him a time or two when he sounded off at the public square and they think that he's competent to handle almost everything. In rural areas, you know, every lawyer is called judge, and they figure if he's called judge, you know, that Judge Ellis over here, he's bound to know just what the law is. Now, that's a problem. And the professional is trying to address himself to that to some degree. For instance, there are some certifications as to whether you can really say that you special-ize in a certain field of law—and this is something that is in vogue now. I don't know how effective it's going to be; it's too early to tell. That may be of some help. The other question is what we've alluded to a time or two—but let me say to you that the bar is working at it. It's not being overlooked. We just don't know what the answers are at the present time and hopefully, the answers can be found. There's much work being done on it. The other is the age-old question and that is how is that individual going to afford today's going rates that a lawyer must charge. Now, let's not blame the legal profession. Let's not say, well, a lawyer has no business charging that much. Everything the lawyer pays for has gone up. I can't begin to tell you how the cost of operating a large law firm has increased. And the same is true of a small one; the same is true of the man who has only one—his own little shop. Everything—the law books that he must acquire, his tools of trade, his secretary's salary, the rent that he pays—everything has gone up and he just can't be a fellow who's going to sit there and practice law at rates that will not permit him to continue. So you do have a real problem. Now, I should say that an effort has been made to try to reach this in several ways. One of the ways has been to see if there's insurance that can be gotten that pays for that sort of matter. And this has been tried in Shreveport, Louisiana, for instance. And there has been some value found in that; it's still questionable. And there are a number of other ways that are now under study—under active study—to try to solve that particular problem. This is where I think the American Bar Association and the other organized groups of our profession can be of tremendous help, and that is to continue to address themselves to the very problems that you raise and if they do not do so, then we're going to have to admit a failure. And the next step, then, is that we're going to have to admit that the system is not working—it just isn't working. All right. Yes?

Male Voice: Mr. Jaworski, are there any kinds of affirmative steps that the bar can take to maintain its independence from the kind of legislative assaults that you spoke about or is the bar going to be limited from now on to being on the defensive?

Jaworski: I'm glad you raised that question. I think an affirmative step that the bar can take is to make sure who goes to the legislature. That is the best way. I'm not condemning the legislature, as such, in its entirety at all. I have a number of friends and a number of people that I greatly admire, and I must also say that I strongly approve of so many young people going to the legislature. The difficulty is that there are some who have had dissatisfactions with the bar for one reason or another and some don't understand fully the operations of the organized bar. Some of them have a chip on their shoulder, very frankly, and they just look upon that as an opportunity to get even with the profession. They feel they have not themselves been particularly successful as lawyers and so they're just going to vent their spleen. Now that's what it amounts to, and it's a rather sad situation. Some of it is a difference in philosophy, but I don't think that they reckon, really, that they fully understand what they're doing to the profession and what they're doing to society by some of the things that they've advocated. When we had our hearings at the time that they were going to shut down on the organized bar in this state, Abner McCall and I both appeared as witnesses. We talked to the committee at length. This was a committee in the Senate which normally is a committee of the more accomplished lawyers than you might find in the House because of the difference in age and so on. And there were several of them there that were just ready to shut down on the bar because of their own personal grievances of one kind or another. But it worked out reasonably well in the end. It wasn't the simplest thing; we were almost sunsetted and almost legislated out of existence. All right, next question. Yes?

Male Voice: You made reference earlier to attorneys advertising. Do you think that there's any form of competition that would be beneficial to the profession that wouldn't be contrary to our code of ethics?

Jaworski: Any form of competition?

Male Voice: Yes. Maybe price competition.

Jaworski: Well, there's not supposed to be a price structure among the organized bar because that would be a violation of antitrust and is something that our friends in Washington would talk about quickly; and at one time, there were suggested fees actually printed and circulated among members of the bar, and that was discontinued because of the claim that this might constitute an effort to engage in unfair price-fixing. I think that the lawyer is going to have to determine for himself what is an appropriate fee. What is an appropriate fee in, let's say, Marlin, Texas, taking a small town close to Waco, may not be an appropriate fee even in Waco. It certainly wouldn't be an appropriate fee in Houston where everything costs a whole lot more. So it would be very difficult to determine that. Secondly, I think that a lawyer who is going to cut his fees too much, I mean, to where he can obviously say that there's something wrong with it, is either starving to death and feels that he has to reach out for whatever he can get, or else his services just are not going to be particularly good. He figures that he can do this job in a short period of time when it may take, in order for it to be done adequately, much longer. That is a very difficult thing to say; we have no comparison of fees in Houston, for instance, except that it's generally known how much is charged per hour for the work that's done. For instance, insurance companies go around and shop to make sure that you don't charge them more per hour than they can get from somebody else they consider to be competent. You do run into that. Let me tell you something about the fixing of a fee. I learned early in the game that this, to me, always is one of the most difficult things you can do. I was practicing here in Waco. Tom Scott, who was a wonderful person and a great lawyer and a very, very dear friend of mine—no longer with us—I was his younger partner. And Tom still liked to go out and play baseball at times; he'd broken his leg. And so I had to try to run the office and a fellow came in from some distance south of here, had left his equipment out on the highway, and somebody ran into it and he was sued. The case involved a fair sum of money in those days. He came in to see us and they called and said he'd come in to talk to us about our employment. And I had talked to Tom Scott about it when I went to the hospital to see him. Tom said, "Well, I'll tell you what you ought to do." After we'd kicked it around a while he said, "You ought to try to get seven hundred and fifty dollars, but if you can't get that," he said, "get five hundred dollars." He said, "don't let him get away because we need it." Well, we did need it because we were—rent was coming around and we were having trouble—needing things, living from hand-to-mouth on top of

58

it. The fellow sat down there, and I talked with him and I tried to fix that fee and I was going to say five hundred and I was so afraid that the thing was going to get away from me that I said two hundred and fifty dollars. He was thrilled to death. He wrote out the check right then and there, and I went back hanging my head to talk to Tom. "Did you get the case yet?" "I got the case all right, working on it already." "What fee'd you get?" It was the hardest thing for me to ever do—to tell Tom that I couldn't say five hundred; I said two-fifty. And I thought Tom was going to break that other leg running after me. But that was a very, very sad experience; it's just that hard to learn how to fix an appropriate fee at times—it really is. In time I could fix some pretty good fees without batting an eye. So it comes through experience, you see. All right, we have time, Dean, I think, for another question or so. Yes?

Male Voice: Mr. Jaworski, what do we do when we get out of law school today—and of course when that happens—what do we do when we go back to our community and we discover that somebody there in the bar is not doing things properly? How do we handle it as a young lawyer in our—in our community, if the other lawyers won't take a hold of it and do something with it?

Jaworski: Well, of course, if he just is a lawyer who doesn't perform well, there isn't too much you can do about that. If he is a lawyer who really has—is doing things that constitute a violation of the Code of Ethics, or a violation of law, you can do something about it. And that is, it should be called to the attention of the grievance committees at that point. It's not a question of doubt with me because if you begin to perform ably and impressively, you're going to find that this lawyer's own acceptance by the public is going to diminish. And it will be less and less. The problem is that so much of what goes on between lawyers is sometimes claimed to result or stem from a feeling of envy or jealousy or such as that. If you demean yourself as you should and work hard at it, there isn't any question but that you will soon put that lawyer in the shade. If he, on the other hand, does things that are really a tremendous embarrassment to the bar or any kind of embarrassment to the bar, and particularly if they involve law violation, you should proceed to call it to the attention of the authorities. All right. Yes, sir?

Male Voice: What do you see as the role of the law student in the organized bar?

Jaworski: Oh, I think it's very important. I tell you, the law students, they read; they talk things over; they debate these issues. I was at one of their meetings in Honolulu just a few weeks ago and I was much impressed with how they conducted the entire meeting, conducted it as well as the American Bar does in the house of delegates meeting. I listened to several of the speeches that were made, pro and con, on issues that were before the student bar and they were just excellent. The talks, the arguments, I thought, were quite impressive. So there is much that you learn by way of training yourself for service in the organized bar at a later date. I also want to say to you that nobody sneers at what the student bar association comes out with. What the law student's association reports to the American Bar is looked upon with considerable study and appreciation these days. There was a time when it wasn't, a number of years ago, but that's not the case now. So it is an important function that can be performed.

I guess our time is about up, Dean. I want to tell you again how nice it was to be with you and I really look forward to the next lectures because we're going to talk about some things that I believe will be of interest inasmuch as you'll be out practicing law before too long, we hope. I think that maybe some of these comments will be helpful to you.

VI

The Lawyer and the Bench

A fundamental right the lawyer must have for the profession to have any value to our democratic processes is complete independence. If the lawyer is to be subservient in the discharge of his obligations, he will not be able to protect the rights accorded the individual under our Constitution. I cannot emphasize too strongly the resistance the Bar must marshal against any encroachment on its complete independence. I cannot state the matter better than did Sir Peter Rawlinson, Her Majesty's Attorney General at the time of the American Bar Association's memorable meeting in London in 1971. Said Sir Peter:

> No more than do Judges now crouch at the foot of the throne or beneath a national standard, so no more does the advocate crouch at the foot of the Judge. For without a complete independence of the advocate, there is no independence of the law and not even a pretense of justice.

A. *The Lawyer's Duty*

The responsibility of the lawyer is clear. It is pointedly expressed in the Code of the American College of Trial Lawyers in these words:

> In his advocacy before a court or other tribunal, a lawyer has the professional obligation to represent every client courageously, vigorously, diligently and with all the skill and knowledge he possesses. It is both the right and duty of the lawyer to present his client's cause fully and properly to insist on an opportunity to do so and to see to it that a complete and accurate case record is made without being deterred by any fear of judicial displeasure or punishment.

But it further provides that during the trial:

> A lawyer should always display a courteous, dignified and respectful

attitude toward the Judge presiding, not for the sake of his person, but for the maintenance of respect for and confidence in the judicial office. The Judge, to render effective such conduct, has reciprocal responsibilities of courtesy to and respect for the lawyer who is also an officer of the court.

B. *The Judge's Duty*

The report and recommendations of the College's Committee on Disruption of the Judicial Process declares that the Judge has the duty "to recognize the obligation of every lawyer to represent his clients courageously and vigorously, and to treat every lawyer with the courtesy and respect due one performing an essential role in the trial process." This monumental work spotlighted the wrong and the futility of disruptive conduct in the courtroom and unmistakably laid bare the restraints the advocate must observe in the trial arena.

Note should also be taken of the provisions of the Canons of Judicial Ethics as adopted by the American Bar Association, which expressly and pointedly placed on the Judge the responsibility of being "patient, dignified and courteous toward litigants, jurors, witnesses, lawyers and others who appear before him." It also imposes on him the responsibility of extending to the advocate the "full right to be heard according to law." One of the qualifications that Socrates in his great wisdom specified for a Judge was "to hear courteously."

C. P. Harvey, Queen's Counsel, in his work, "The Advocate's Devil," well described one of the types of judges the Bar at times has to tolerate. In the words of Harvey, he spoke of a

> marvelously quickwitted judge, with a superb command of the English language, with a vast knowledge of public affairs and with a flair for advocacy which had brought him to the front rank of law and politics. He lacked only the one quality which should distinguish a judge: that of being judicial. He remained the perpetual advocate. The opening of a case had only to last for five minutes before one could feel—and sometimes actually see—which side he had taken; thereafter, the other side had no chance.

All of which reminds me of an experience a friend of mine had in the courtroom when faced by a judge who proceeded to take away from him the interrogation of a witness and to become an advocate in the process. My lawyer friend sweated the proceeding for a few minutes and finally interrupted the judge to say, "Your Honor, I don't mind your trying my case for me—just please don't lose it."

C. *The Professional Relationship*

It has been said that a bad Bench makes for a bad Bar. But as pointed out by Queen's Counsel Harvey, "At all events the advocate should avoid quarreling with the judge." I think that we can all agree that quarrels should be avoided, but never should the advocate fail fully and courageously to represent his client's cause because he happens to face an oppressive and quarrelsome judge. Here the important element is that the lawyer should never flinch from presenting the cause to its full worth—at the same time living up to his own responsibilities as an officer of the court.

If you will pardon the injection of a personal experience, I once told a federal judge—a crusty one of tyrannical instincts—after he had indicated he would not disturb the status quo, that his failure to grant an injunction would create chaos in the wholesale arrests of truck operators. While speaking these words to the judge, one of my colleagues was frantically tugging at my coattail to get me to sit down. He was in horror of the thought of my spending the night in jail. But when I spoke these words, I did it courteously, though firmly. The judge and I looked each other in the eye while my colleague almost passed out. The judge reversed his earlier indication and granted the restraining order without further comment or proceeding.

This brings me to the obligation of the Bar to participate in the providing of an appropriate judicial selection process. It is to be deplored that in our state system we do not have a method of judicial selection and tenure similar to what has been termed the "Missouri Plan." The elective system, in instances of judicial offices, has particular shortcomings not present in other elections. The prime difficulty, of course, is that the average voter has no way of judging the qualifications of the candidate and seldom even undertakes to discuss his abilities and character with lawyers who are acquainted with the individual office seeker. Most of the voters do not even know the names of judges on the appellate courts who are in office, and many do not know the names of their local judges. The result is blind voting—and frequently there is merely a selection of a popular name—one that has been heard before. I hope that before long our State Bar will sponsor a process of selection that avoids the difficulties and complexities I have just mentioned. In the past, one of the problems has been that the plaintiff's Bar is fearful that a set of judges selected by a commission process or ultimately selected by the Governor may be influenced by the defendant's Bar. This is a mistaken notion and has been proved to be so. As the matter now stands, both the plaintiff's Bar and the defendant's Bar make large campaign contributions in races and this is not a salutary condition. Whether the present mode of election of judges is to continue or whether a change is made, it is the clear duty of lawyers to participate in the process and to assist in the selection of the best qualified candidates.

On the federal level, the American Bar Association has actively participated in the screening of judges. In recent years commissions have been assisting in the selection of judges to serve on the courts of appeals. In the selection of trial judges in the federal system, Senators have been soliciting the assistance of the Bar and inviting the Bar's expressions. As to the Supreme Court of the United States, the American Bar Association, through its Federal Judiciary Committee, also expresses its views on the qualifications of judges. There is much that is to be said in regard to the importance of these functions, but due to the limited time available, I must pretermit any elaboration. But I cannot emphasize too strongly the great importance of the Bar interesting itself actively in the judicial selection process so as to make certain that judges of ability, character and industry grace the Bench. It has been aptly said that "the quality of our Judges is the quality of our justice."

I do not want to end this phase of my remarks without stressing, with the greatest of emphasis, the obligation the advocate has to demean himself respectfully and with the utmost propriety in the courtroom at all times. There is no place for lawyer misconduct in the courtroom. If he or she is imposed upon improperly by the judge, there is ample opportunity to effectively, yet courteously, state in the record the objections and exceptions to the court's conduct. It has been my observation that the appellate courts will not side with the trial judge unduly—on the contrary, if the trial judge has misbehaved, the appellate court is quick to point it out with certainty. The goal of judge and advocate alike should be to achieve what Mr. Justice Sutherland of the United States Supreme Court termed "the calm spirit of regulated justice."

QUESTIONS AND ANSWERS

Male Voice: You said that one of the duties of the Supreme Court was to try to guarantee equal justice under the law and you said that in recent history they hadn't done that at times. And, I wonder if you had an example.

Jaworski: Well, let me just tell you what I mean by that. And I'm not particularly criticizing the Court for it; I don't know what the answer to it is. There isn't any question that the United States Supreme Court in recent years and for quite some time, as a matter of fact, for a long time, through most of its history, has taken hold of questions that have been related to social issues and have really engaged in legislation. Where Congress should have acted and didn't act, the Supreme Court stepped in and said, well, this is going to be the law of the land. Now, has it been for good or has it been for bad? Certainly, in many of the instances, it's been for good. But, it doesn't change the fact that the Supreme Court, instead of just merely interpreting the Constitution, actually begins to make law, itself, in a sense of providing an answer to some of the social problems that face the country. I have never been one who has condemned the Supreme Court for doing it, because I have felt that in most of the instances, it was due to a failure on the part of Congress to act. What I have thought is that they have tortured the due process clause at times. They would bring just about everything under the fourteenth amendment and I thought that this was, perhaps, straining what the fourteenth amendment was intended for. And we'll get to that; for instance, whether you can have television in a courtroom. We'll discuss that a little bit later on.

Male Voice: Sir, there is a growing concern about the usurpation of legislative lawmaking power. How do you view this situation? Do you feel that there are sufficient checks and balances on political behavior?

Jaworski: In presenting Justice Lewis Powell for the Great Leader's Award that the Southwestern Legal Foundation gives on occasions, just a few months ago, I made reference to that very subject. And here's what I said about it—this is just my own reaction to it. And there's been criticism of our United States Supreme Court for going into matters that relate to fields that Congress should be addressing itself to. And you frequently say that the Supreme Court has turned itself into a superlegislature. Well, again, that the Supreme Court has done, perhaps, some legislating, is not to be denied, but where does the fault lie? Just where does the fault lie? If the Congress of the United States is not going to address itself to some subjects that are very important and do involve some individual rights, why should not the United States Supreme Court address itself to it? I think that by and large it has worked out pretty well. I am not happy over some of the decisions; I'm not particularly pleased with how the due process approbation has been stretched on the fourteenth amendment, because I think it's a little dangerous for it to be continually stretched to meet almost any situation that arises. But on the other hand, I just feel that the occasion arises when the United States Supreme Court must take the bit in the mouth and must act. I think it was Justice Holmes who always contended that law really was experience—that's what law is based on. And this really accounts for there being so many instances in which the courts take hold of a new matter because experience—experience is taught and it's necessary for the courts to take a look at it. The experience of society has brought it to the courts. So, I must say to you that it's easy to sit there and postulate on the subject that the Supreme Court ought to stay away from doing any legislating, and then you begin to think about some of the problems that the Supreme Court's come to grips with that may have not been handled by the legislature, by Congress. And then you begin to find that your criticism weakens and that's about as much as I can say on it; that's my own reaction to it. Yes, sir.

Male Voice: Much earlier you had made reference to the contempt citations and the behavior of some people who were in contempt of court and the lawyer's role in it. My question is, in cases where a reporter—a news reporter—is placed in jail for contempt for failure to reveal sources, such as the case in The University of Texas' situation, wherein the issuance of the contempt citation and the reporter's refusal to turn over information or sources or what-have-you, may involve some constitutional question—What would be your reaction to—and I notice these reporters often wave these contempt citations around like a flag, you know, and right proud of it and all this, but, notwithstanding that type of behavior, what would be your reaction to, say, a lawyer who would be schooled in media law that would take the reporter's view on the constitutional question?

Jaworski: I think that if there's a constitutional question of law, I think if he's acting in good faith and he believes that his constitutional rights are being violated, he's taking the proper step—in submitting himself to a contempt order, he's held in contempt of court and what happens, he appeals his case to a higher court. I had the experience a number of years ago, where the district court of an outlying town near Houston, entered an order saying that "the Houston newspapers will not print anything relating to a certain trial that we're going to have in this county, because following it I have a companion case, and I just don't want my jurors disqualified. So, I don't want your newspapers which are carried into this county to carry anything on that subject." And what we did was we advised our clients that the only way the matter could be adjudicated by the higher courts was for them to let themselves be held in contempt. Now, this was for the purpose of testing the rule of law. What is it ultimately to be? And I find nothing wrong with that. By the same token, you don't need a whole bunch of fellows to do it at one time. One person can do it and contest the constitutionality of a law; you don't have wholesale violations by hundreds or thousands as this has happened sometimes in the past. Now, to get back to your question, I think that if this man really, genuinely believes that his constitutional rights are being violated that he should let the case be decided by the higher courts. And the only way that he can do it is to let a contempt order be entered by his refusing to abide by it. But everyone understands that, and understands the reasons why it's done and that way a habeas corpus writ is sued out and then the case is, in time, determined by the Court of Criminal Appeals. This is what happened in our particular case. I think if the young man in Austin believes truly that his constitutional rights have been violated then he has the right to do that. I don't want to get into any local arguments over here, but I do draw a distinction between that situation and that which happened here, simply because you have a matter here, where actually the one running the newspaper is the university itself, and you have to take that into account, and let's not get off on that one.

VII

The Challenge of the Future

On the horizon appear several challenges the profession faces in current times and will continue to face for the foreseeable future. Let me list a few of the more significant—then briefly discuss them.

A. *The Problems of the Profession*

(1) An answer must be found, at least partly, to the problem of providing needed services to that large segment of our society unable to qualify as poor yet unable to pay the going price for a lawyer's help.

(2) Delays in trials, both criminal and civil but especially criminal, are far too long in many jurisdictions. This failing has plagued our justice system for many generations. We must not permit it to worsen and must strive to improve it.

I will repeat what I said a few years ago: In many jurisdictions, the criminal justice system is creaking and creeping and is sorely in need of overhauling. In some jurisdictions, witnesses are imposed upon and become discouraged because of delays and unfair treatment; prospective jurors become exhausted from delays and indifferent handling; some defendants are caused to languish in jail for all too long and without the benefit of rehabilitation; underpaid prosecutors are disheartened and some are too inexperienced to properly discharge the responsibilities they undertake; defense counsels score triumphs at the expense of antiquated procedures—and the end result is that society is the heavy loser.

I had occasion recently to read the report of the president of the Association of the Bar of the City of New York. He was writing of the reformation that faced the profession. I do not think that he has exaggerated the situation—in fact, I thought well enough of his comments to pass them on to you. Here is what he concluded:

The important reformation will come in finding ways to relieve the adversary system from burdens it cannot carry, nor was ever meant to carry: judicial inertia; the achievement of complete racial desegregation; the management of schools and busing; the oversight of penal institutions; jurisdiction over victimless crimes; pre-censorship of books, plays and television; review of administrative determinations in the field of science, the environment and the uses of energy; "fault" as a judicable issue; administration of estates and the regulation of marital problems; the enormously costly and time-consuming "discovery" procedures, etc.

The adversary system cannot carry these and many other burdens. The system has, at least since Dickens' time, been subject to inordinate systemic delay in the final disposition of cases that has not responded to symptomatic remedies. The system constantly grows more costly. Only the very rich can afford that cost. The system is creating a huge bureaucracy of judges, masters and supporting personnel that cannot be controlled by ordinary management techniques.

(3) Bar Associations everywhere are increasing demands on their members to meet their "public interest responsibilities," and this undoubtedly will continue for some time to come. Not too much progress has been made, but as events determine the greater need for such services, the Bar will have to find a way of coming to grips with this need.

(4) I recall that in 1972, during my term as president of the American Bar Association, grave concerns were expressed as to how our society would absorb the large number of law school graduates and how the profession should prepare itself for the influx of many thousands of new lawyers. The concern was so grave that I was caused to appoint a Task Force on Professional Utilization. Here were the problems that the Task Force were to address itself to: ". . . How can more lawyers be utilized, economically and meaningfully, in the traditional spheres of practice? How can the present lawyer maldistribution as between urban centers and small cities be adjusted? What can the law schools do to channel students into such emerging and less crowded specialties as environmental law, criminal law, poverty law and consumer law? What new opportunities lie in public administration and in serving the millions of low and middle income citizens who rarely or never seek a lawyer's services? Are additional law schools needed? What are the prospects for new specialties, and what adjustments will be necessary in law schools' curricula?" I remarked then that:

Some of these are new questions never really considered before. No doubt many others will arise, including the question of arbitrary restriction of law school enrollments. Actually, law schools already are imposing restrictions necessitated by the limitations of their capacity. In other respects ours always has been an open profession, and I hope it always can be.

Moreover, we know that the demand for legal services is growing and that prepaid legal services, government-supported legal assistance programs and other developments not now foreseeable are likely to enlarge lawyer employment opportunities in the future, so that any attempt to establish a ceiling on the number of lawyers needed would be highly conjectural, apart from the questions of necessity or desirability of such a step.

These were my views then and they are very much the same today.

(5)   I still have a deep concern about the attitude of indifference to the preservation of the profession as one of high trust and great honor, exhibited not only by lawyers who have practiced at the Bar for years, but by some who are entering the profession in current times. For the profession to continue to have an important place in our society and for it to improve its stature in the public eye, it is indispensable that the law schools teach courses in ethics and punctuate the time-tested, traditional characteristics of the profession and the role the lawyer has played in the development of our democratic institutions and in the prestige our country has attained in the world. There should be inculcated a fervency in every law student and every law graduate similar to what Daniel Webster described of his own feelings in an address he delivered to the Charleston, South Carolina Bar in 1847. Here are his words:

> I love our common profession, and love all who honor it. I regard it as the great ornament, and one of the chief defenses and securities of our institutions. It is indispensable to and conservative of public liberty. I honor it from the bottom of my heart. If I am anything it is the law, that notable profession, that sublime science which we all pursue, that has made me what I am. It has been my ambition, coeval with my early manhood, nay with my youth, to be thought worthy to be ranked under the banner of that profession.

Let me briefly mention a few other challenges that appear on the horizon and that the profession must face in the oncoming years. Some of these challenges are with us now and have been for some period of time. Others are becoming more acute. Time will not permit me to elaborate on these, but they are worthy of your consideration.

(6)   Our penal institutions need improvement.

(7)   The lawyer needs to return to leadership in his locality. This is true whether he practices in a hamlet or in a metropolis.

(8)   The Bar by its own organized efforts must project a better professional image—both as to ability and as to ethical conduct.

(9)   There must be a greater degree of participation in the legislative halls, in fact in the entire political process, to avoid engulfment in

71

masses of statutes and regulations which make it difficult to give sound advice at reasonable costs.

(10) The screening process of those admitted to the practice of law must continue to emphasize moral character as well as educational requirements. In some jurisdictions there has not been sufficient emphasis on moral character.

B. *A Personal Challenge*

I have often been asked what my greatest experience was in the practice of law—which one gave me the greatest personal satisfaction—which of the efforts of mine gave me the greatest thrill. Well, I will take a few minutes to tell you about it. I have never before discussed it publicly. You may be wondering whether I will speak of the thrill that came from the United States Supreme Court's opinion resulting in a triumph over the President of the United States in obtaining the Watergate tapes. Well, that was not it. Neither was it the time a number of years ago when I received for my law firm a million dollar fee as a result of the successful disposition of a will contest. This was when a million dollars still had a value of a million dollars. This one was not a personal triumph—it served to show the strength of our system of justice. Let me tell you about it.

One afternoon in 1958, my pastor called and said he had to see me on an urgent matter. I told him to come at once.

"There's a real tragedy," he said as he walked into my office. He told me the Court of Criminal Appeals of Texas that morning had affirmed the death sentence of a man convicted of murder—yet the man was not responsible for what he had done.

"His brother is a great servant of the Lord's," my pastor continued. "He's one of the most dedicated Presbyterian ministers in Texas." Then my pastor told me how broken-hearted his fellow minister was. Other lawyers suggested that my pastor come to me. The family had no money, but they needed help. I asked if the condemned man had a lawyer, and my pastor said he had. He said the lawyer knew I was being consulted and agreed that I should be. Then he told me as much about the case as he knew. The man had been convicted of murdering his elderly mother-in-law. He had beaten her brutally with a vase, had been arrested on the day of the murder and had made a written confession. Local feeling ran high against him. Fourteen days after his arrest he was tried.

His only defense was insanity. He had been discharged from the Air Force because of mental problems, but the records of his discharge could not be found before the trial. His defense of insanity could not be fully

72

developed. So the poor demented man had been sentenced to death and the Court of Criminal Appeals had affirmed it.

My first reaction was to discourage my pastor from pursuing the matter further. I pointed to the action of the Court of Criminal Appeals in having affirmed the sentence and of my now being asked to in effect "shut the gate after the horses are out." After my pastor rather pointedly told me that he was leaving the matter in my hands and that it was now between me and the Lord, I decided to take it on and do my best. Other pressing matters had to be put aside because of the exigency of the situation. I filed a strong brief with the Court in support of the motion for rehearing. There was a long wait. The Court came down with a new opinion, although only one judge dissented from the conviction. There I still faced a 2-1 upholding of the death sentence, but I had something of a new lease on life in view of the writing of the new opinion. I prepared a second motion for rehearing and then came another long wait. The Court came down with another opinion, this time reversing the conviction by a vote of 2-1.

After the reversal, I met with the district attorney who had prosecuted the case and he became convinced of the insanity of the defendant. He joined in the holding of a proceeding to determine the defendant's mental condition and the jury returned a finding of insanity. I had the good Lord's help, I can assure you, for this final outcome was the answer to the prayers of many, including my own. But the ending also served as tribute to our system of justice.

C. *Predictions for the Future*

In these lectures, I have been turning back the pages of my personal experiences at the Bar for fifty plus years. I have polished my crystal ball—still, some of it continues in a murky state. What are my prognostications?

The trial of cases will remain an art and regardless of so-called procedural reforms, the fundamentals of good advocacy will not change. It is not unlikely that due to congestion in litigation and perhaps other factors, there will be a procedural streamlining of trials resulting in the removing of some of the drama, suspense and showmanship still present, primarily in criminal cases. Forensics will continue to play a significant role in some contests, thus bowing to the anguished cry of Judah Benjamin, Confederate Attorney General serving in the administration of Jefferson Davis—"The Daniel Webster type of trial lawyer is as dead as a doornail." Peck added:

> During the intervening 30 odd years, I have often recalled that observation and wondered if the trial lawyer, like his illustrious

prototype, was not fading from the scene.

Anomalous as it is, the last three decades, the period of greatest growth in the law and law practice, have witnessed a decline approaching evaporation in trial practice save in the single area of personal injury litigation.

I do not fully agree with these observations. I still see a place for the "Daniel Webster" type of trial lawyer in some criminal cases. I also see a fair amount of major litigation still in progress in different parts of the country other than personal injury litigation. And this should continue for the forseeable future.

Some law firms in New York and in Chicago, for example, do not handle the defense of personal injury suits—still, they maintain a sizeable trial department. My projection for the foreseeable future would be that there will always be a substantial amount of major litigation in all parts of the country (other than personal injury litigation) although the nature of it may change in time. Who would have thought ten years ago that there would be as many malpractice suits filed against doctors, lawyers, accountants, etc., as are in the courts today? Because of the high cost of litigation as well as delays in reaching the trial of cases, there will be an increased tendency toward settlements without litigation.

I do not look for administrative law on the national level to continue its leaping advances much longer. At some point before many seasons pass, we will heed Madison's wisdom that it is our obligation to make the government control itself. When we do, I hope that the reaction will not be one of the pendulum swinging too far in the opposite direction. There is a significant place in our society for administrative law—properly conceived and established. People engaged in small business, in large business, and even in assisting nonprofit organizations eventually will tire of the inexcusably monumental and burdensome regulations from Washington.

The legal profession must do and will do a better job of disciplining its members. If not, the task will be taken over by state authorities. I have severely criticized the Ethics Committee in Congress for their faint-hearted handling of disciplinary breaches by their members. The legal profession, in many instances, is guilty of the same protectionism.

Because the rule of law is the foundation of our society, there will always be a need for lawyers. Those who prepare themselves well for the practice of the profession, apply their learning diligently, widen their intellectual horizon as they labor and take pride in their work will be rewarded with a full measure of success. It was said years ago that the law is a jealous mistress, and you will find this to be largely true in the early years of your practice.

New fields of law will rise. Some of them have appeared on the scene in recent years, and more are sure to follow. Of relatively recent vintage, in addition to civil rights, are laws relating to products liability and the environment. Only recently, I read of courses in Federal Indian Law and Patient's Rights; Poverty Law and a new approach to Juvenile Justice have also made their appearances.

Before long, class actions will not abound as they have in recent years. Such actions have become good pickings for some lawyers with the unseen "members" of the so-called class winding up with a few crumbs—sometimes with none. Courts will inspect these actions with increased care and concern.

More and more law graduates will go to the smaller communities where they will become "big ducks in little ponds." This is truly a delightful way to practice law and in time to become a leader in the community.

Which way should you go? To the large city—practice on your own, in a small firm, in a medium firm or a large firm? I would not advise going to a large city without an association. You may wind up using food stamps. I fear that I am not an impartial judge when it comes to passing on the size of the firm to join in a large city. I will say parenthetically, however, that it is one whale of a thrill to start in an office resembling a cubby hole and wind up in one of the more sumptuous in the entire assembly.

There is something about practicing in a small city or in a town that cannot be duplicated in a metropolis. The mad rush is absent—there is usually more camaraderie among lawyers—outside of the courtroom, to be sure. There is a difference in the practice, and the average client often is friend and neighbor to the lawyer. As I struggled through the maze of complexities in Houston, both in professional and in private life, I more than once took a wistful glance in the direction of Waco.

What technology will do in changing the practice is difficult to foretell. The searching and digging for a case in point is a thing of the past. All types of new gadgets and computers do much of the work in our offices now. Fewer and fewer secretaries can take shorthand. No one heard of paralegal clerks until a few years ago, and now our offices are filled with them. Law firms use summer law clerks from many of the law schools now upon completion of their second year. Most of them seem to know much more now than most of us did after completing law school. Wherever you go—whatever will be your specialty—there will always be ample opportunity for the achiever.

In recent years there has been a greater awareness of the need of *pro bono publico* services, and response of law firms and lawyers to this need increased in the past decade. I believe that there is much more of this type of work done than is recorded. Many members of the Bar help quietly and without ostentation as the individual's need for help arises. Every lawyer should be willing to lend a helping hand when need arises within the limitations of his own circumstances. This should continue to be a matter of conscience with him or her. Attempts to put such services on an organized basis may not meet with substantial success. Recently, the ABA Commission on Evaluation of Professional Standards reaffirmed its belief that lawyers should be required to perform free public interest legal service but dropped the requirement for annual reporting of such services.

My greatest concern for the future of the profession arises from the advertisements by lawyers, spawned as a result of the United States Supreme Court's decision. At best, it is a cheapening exercise. At worst, it should be odious to every worthy lawyer. Advertising may explode uncontrolled, even in this state. The lawyers of Texas so far have not voted a program of control. The last effort failed to produce enough participants in the voting for the election to count. I believe, however, that after a period of wild advertising, the pendulum will swing back. The public will soon learn to pay little attention to these self-serving representations. There may even be more malpractice suits—even false advertising charges against lawyers, and these may serve to cure the advertisers from rampant advertising.

The prediction I am about to make probably will surprise you. I believe that there will be an increased use of television in the courtroom and that eventually it will be considered appropriate for use in most legal proceedings. There will have to be some restrictions and limitations on an *ad hoc* basis, and the rights of the accused as to fairness of trial will need to be respected, of course.

The United States Supreme Court several years ago in the case of *Estes v. Texas*[8] held that the circumstances of that case were such as to have denied due process to the defendant because of the use of television. The decision was by a vote of 5-4, and Mr. Justice Harlan indicated doubt and uncertainty in his vote with the majority, making it clear that he was going along with the holding only because of the particular facts of the case. Actually, the pre-trial proceedings were so burdened and impeded with television paraphernalia that the participants in the trial were handicapped in performing their various functions. Cables were strung all over the courtroom and television cameras were constantly in the way of those who were conducting the trial proceedings. Later, during the trial itself, the television camera was hidden from view and the lens did its work through a small hole in the rear of the courtroom. There was no visible sign of any television equipment. The jurors executed affidavits

[8]381 U.S. 532, 85 S. Ct. 1628, 14 L. Ed. 2d 543 (1965).

stating that they were not even aware of the presence of the television camera. The court, however, ignored any reference to these facts in its opinion and stressed only the extreme circumstances that existed at the pre-trial hearing. This made it all the more obvious to those of us familiar with the facts that several of the Justices on the Court were determined to hand down a decision that would serve to bar television from the courtroom regardless of how it was used. Mr. Justice Harlan's joinder with the majority was on such narrow premise, however, that it is quite unlikely that a majority of the Court would render a similar decision were the issue to come up before it at this time. It is well known, of course, that Chief Justice Burger very much dislikes the presence of television even when he is making a public address. I happen to know, however, that this is based primarily on his problem with temporary blindness caused by the bright lights shining in his direction. What his views would be about the use of the camera in the courtroom, I do not profess to know. I do believe that a majority would be inclined at this time to permit the cameras to be used to a greater degree than was true during the days of the Warren Court when due process was stretched to meet almost every desire of the Court.

At the request of the then Attorney General of Texas, I served as Special Assistant Attorney General for the State of Texas in the preparation of the briefs and in the presentation of oral argument of that case in the United States Supreme Court. It is my belief that the principal reason the Court overturned the conviction was due to the fear that future televising of courtroom proceedings would impact adversely on the public's image of the administration of justice. The American Bar Association had been taking a strong stand in opposition to the use of television as had other organizations of the legal profession. Two of the Justices who sat in the case had openly denounced the use of television. Mr. Justice Douglas, one of the two, had written articles strongly opposing the use of television.

Actually, I felt, as did others, that Mr. Justice Douglas should not have sat in this case after having theretofore committed himself to a definite and what seemed to be an irreversible position on the subject of televising courtroom proceedings. Mr. Justice Clark had not been as outspoken on the subject, but his views adverse to the use of television were quite well known because he had confided them to a number of individuals. It was interesting to note that the American Bar Association took the extreme position that the use of a television camera in the courtroom was *per se* illegal and unconstitutional. The Supreme Court did not adopt this view.

In recent times the American Bar Association's House of Delegates again considered the question. There was not too much debate on it, although in the end the Association stayed by its former position. The vote was not by a wide margin, and I believe that the next time the matter comes up before the House of Delegates of the American Bar Association, the longstanding position of the Association will be changed. I did not take any part of the consideration of this matter at the recent debate because of my involvement in the *Estes* case.

A number of experiments have been conducted in courtrooms that have negated some of the fears that have been previously stressed. In addition, the limited use of television has been approved by several states. The trend is to the acceptance of television in more and more jurisdictions. I believe that ultimately the matter should rest with the sound discretion of the presiding judge. I do not believe that a hard and fast rule can be laid down that would admit the use of television under all conditions or alternatively eliminate television in all proceedings. Each factual situation must be judged on the basis of the constitutional rights of the parties affected by the proceeding. What may be entirely appropriate and constitutional in one proceeding may, *per force* other circumstances, become an invasion of the constitutional rights of participants in another.

The profession will never be a popular one in the public eye. Why not, you may ask. Nowhere do I find the answer to this question better stated than in an address delivered by former Chief Justice John E. Hickman of the Supreme Court of Texas in an address to the American Bar Association in 1952. These are his words:

> Of course, the lawyers as a whole can never be popular. They represent minority groups and stand for individual rights. They must place themselves athwart the current of public opinion when waves of prejudice roll. There always have been and doubtless will be gibes and disparaging remarks hurled at our profession. We should not be overly concerned about that, but should be concerned about rekindling a resolve to overcome and smother them by lives of rectitude and public service.

Dedicated lawyers, devoted to the profession of law, of high moral and ethical standards always will occupy an important and admired place in our society. This is inescapably true because this type of lawyer in the practice of his profession will be serving the public interest. He will be playing a prominent part in fashioning the rules of conduct for the welfare of our society. What other profession is privileged to make a greater contribution?

Old lawyers who have been through the mill are liberal with their advice to law students and to young lawyers. I am reminded of one given by John W. Griggs who served as Attorney General under William McKinley just before the 20th Century. Here is what he said:

So I urge you not to strive exclusively for the pecuniary rewards of your profession, but to look forward to a career of influence and usefulness that shall include your neighborhood, your State, your Country, within its beneficent reach. For your example let me commend the ideal of the good lawyer—I do not say the great, but the good lawyer—an ideal that has been realized in the life of every substantial city and court, especially in the older neighborhoods; a man of kindly and benignant disposition, friendly alike with his well-to-do and his poorer fellow townsmen, acquainted with their habits and individual history, and with a pretty accurate notion of their opinions and prejudices as well as their ways and means; genial and sociable, yet dignified and self-contained; of staid and comfortable appearance; in manner alert; in conversation always moderate and respectful; shrewd in his observations, wise, but with perennial humor and love of pleasantry; as a citizen always concerned and active in the interests of his town, his state and his country; not an agitator, nor a perpetual fault-finder, nor giving out the intimation that he is better or wiser than others; but ready to confer, to adjust, to agree, to get the best possible, if not the utmost that is desirable; to him the people turn in local emergencies for guidance and counsel on their public affairs—even partisanship fearing not to trust to his honor and wisdom; so free from all cause of offense that there is no tongue to lay a word against his pure integrity—too dignified and respectful to tempt familiarity; too genial and generous to provoke envy or jealousy; revered by his brethren of the bar; helpful and kindly to the young; in manners suave and polite, with a fine courtliness of the old flavor—what Carendon described in John Hampden as "a flowing courtesy toward all men."

If you do all of this, you will meet the measure of the ideal lawyer, but again, you and your family may darn well starve to death.

QUESTIONS AND ANSWERS

Leon Jaworski: Now I want to say to you that it has been a great experience to give you this very last lecture. We have approximately twenty minutes for questions, if you care to ask any. Remember now, this is your last opportunity. And if I can shed any light on what is on your mind, I shall attempt to do so.

Female Voice: Mr. Jaworski, you mentioned in your lecture that in the future that trial lawyers might possibly play a smaller role. I just wondered, how do you personally feel about that possibility?

Jaworski: Of a trial lawyer playing a smaller role—well, actually it may be that the trial of cases will not be as many and may not be as prominent a part of the practice of the legal profession in a number of years as they are today. This depends very much upon what is done by way of reforming some of the delays, the high cost of litigation, so that we don't find ourselves confronted with a change that is brought about because of the necessities of expensive litigation, especially in serving those who simply cannot pay the rate. If there is no change or if the reforms and the changes are such as to take care of some of the burdens that exist now, then obviously there's no reason to anticipate that there will be any less litigation. And personally I hope that there will be found the answers to some of the problems that beset us now and that there will be a continuance of the application of the adversary system which as you recall, I've from the very outset said that I believe it is better than any other. Now, there was a hand up back there. Yes, sir?

Male Voice: How do you think the recent developments in commercial free speech, in particular advertising for attorneys, will affect the image of attorneys in society?

Jaworski: I am just sick over it, very frankly, the idea of there being advertising. To me, it's something that I just did not believe would come to pass. We had always thought that a lawyer who went out and solicited business was guilty of a gross violation of ethics. I'm not quarrelling with the Supreme Court's decision; maybe this was a decision that had to be rendered as it was and perhaps, if I had the responsibility of rendering a decision, would have come down as they did. But it is regrettable, and I wish that the profession did not exercise any advertising. I do point out that I believe that we may be digging our own graves if we go too far with the matter of advertising, because I think there is a good chance that it will boomerang and it will actually hurt, may even lead to some malpractice suits. But in any event, I can just say to you that I regret it very much. I wish that lawyers did not advertise. I think that there's very little good that can be found in the practice of advertising. There is much opportunity for a person to be misguided. I'm not saying that that isn't true today. One goes into a law office that has a shingle hanging on the outside and the individual, the prospective client, thinks that he or she is being served by an able lawyer. They have a right to so conclude and that is not always the case—but that is the responsibility of the profession. If the profession properly cleans its house, that won't be the case. The lawyer is either competent to handle a matter or he's going to refer it to some other lawyer who is competent to do so. We'll get into the details of that a little bit more later. The next question, yes?

Male Voice: Arbitration has become more and more prevalent in the legal system today with revenues. I was wondering what you thought the role of arbitration and attorneys in arbitration would be in the future?

Jaworski: It's a very good question. It's something the legal profession has to face. If we don't find a way of avoiding the high cost of litigation and the delays in litigation, you're going to see more and more arbitration. There's no need in guessing about it. It's a foregone conclusion that it will happen. Arbitration is beginning to be thought of, and I think will become more significant; it will be resorted to more often than in the past and there'll be new vehicles set up in order to avoid the high cost of litigation and the long delays. Yes, sir?

Female Voice: Mr. Jaworski, as future lawyers, what do you feel law schools and individual students can do to best to equip themselves in the practice of law?

Jaworski: Well, what can law schools and what can the individual student do to equip himself or herself for the practice of law? That's a very good question. I do want to say that I think that law schools today are doing a much better job of preparing the student for the practice of law than at any time that I know anything about. And they're infinitely better than the days when I went to law school. And I think there has been an upgrading; there has been a preparation that is absolutely amazing. Now, when a young lawyer comes into a law office having just graduated from law school, he's of real use—of real benefit. The Dean and I were talking earlier. It used to be in my day that when a young lawyer graduated from law school, he was looked upon as a liability for the first year and he was paid accordingly. He got seventy-five dollars a month and the secretary got a hundred dollars a month. So, that's about the way it was. The situation is quite different, and your obligations, your responsibilities as a lawyer are being pointed up more in law school today, and I think that there's going to be still some more upgrading in that respect. I feel that there's just—every effort should be made to have the student leaving the law school feel deep down in his own heart that he's a member of a noble profession and he's got to live that sort of a life and practice law accordingly.

Male Voice: Yes, Mr. Jaworski, you talked about some of the fears and problems that might arise by bringing television into the court. Do you feel that there are any benefits that can be derived there?

Jaworski: Yes, I do. There are great benefits, and of course, there are also some losses. I think much depends upon how it's handled, how it's regulated. First, of course, comes the proper application of the discretion of the judge. Secondly, the news media itself will have to be cooperative, will have to exercise good restraint and judgment itself. You can see where this matter could be one that could operate as a detriment, in fact an invasion of the rights of the accused in some cases or an invasion of the rights perhaps of even of individuals in cases other than criminal cases. I think that the great value is that there are many myths that circulate about our system of justice. I have seen a case proceed from the beginning to end; from the time that a jury was selected until the very end, so that it was a great credit to our system of justice. I've also seen some things done that were rather sloppily done. I think that once the television enters the courtroom you're going to find an absence of some of these sloppy handling of matters in the courtroom. I think you'll find that judges will shape up. And others will do their job much better. So, it has had educational features and also that very helpful feature of change. There are some instances, it's true, where the witnesses testifying would feel they are inhibited, perhaps; and that's bad. At the beginning, undoubtedly, some lawyers would perhaps put on a little bit more of a show if they knew they were on television than they would otherwise. I think those things would take care of themselves in time. And remember that with the advanced technology now, they are able to place a camera in the back that can't be seen by witness, lawyer, or juror or anybody else. It can be done on a very, very high plane scientifically. That doesn't alter the fact that the witness may know that there's going to be a televising and that others will be hearing of his or her testimony throughout the households, and it may be that this will be something that may affect that particular witness, certainly feeling that her own or his own privacy has been invaded. It gets down to determining what is right and what is best to accommodate our system of justice and primarily, has there been lack of due process of law; has there really been an invasion of the rights of the accused? So, I think that these questions are going to be settled; I think that with careful handling it's going to be very difficult to say that there actually has been an invasion of due process of law. Let me say to you that today I have found that on occasions the conduct—when it's been a very, very prominent trial, the conduct of—of members of the press, and I don't blame them, but it's just a fact of life—running around the courtroom, constantly asking you and buttonholing you during the recess for information, and otherwise milling around, cause more of a distraction than does this camera way back in the end of the courtroom. So, you know it's very easy to get excited over the use of television. But when you analyze it more carefully, I think that you don't find the objection that some people raise. All right, I'll take the next question. Yes, sir?

Male Voice: Sometimes it seems like those who encourage *pro bono*, at least in the large firms with the greatest resources—I know a lot of the firms that come to Baylor, their policy on *pro bono* is that they don't discourage *pro bono* as long as it doesn't interfere with your work in the firm and they can do it on their own time, while some of the Eastern firms are actually going so far as establishing *pro bono* departments in their firms—What do you think is the role of the firm—of the large firm rather than the individual lawyer in encouraging *pro bono*?

Jaworski: Yes, that's a subject that's not easy to answer and much of the criticism that you mention does have a basis. Here's your problem: You have a large firm to be sectionalized and you have some lawyers, as I have covered with you before, who do nothing but say for instance, tax work, or let's say they do nothing but energy work and they've become specialists in this field. And along comes a fellow who needs to be represented, let's say, in a proceeding that involved an aggravated assault or such as that who wants to file a suit for damages. Are you going to take an energy lawyer or are you going to take one whose entire limitations have related to his entire work as related to matters of taxes, for instance? That's been the circumvention of his whole efforts—and take him and let him handle the case of that kind. No, you don't. In the first place, he or she can't do it properly and secondly, you have not served properly the client that needs to be helped. This is one of the big problems. Now, you just can't take a law firm and say well, we're going to make one tenth of all of those across the board here available for *pro bono.* There is more *pro bono* work done by the law firms than you know. There are no records kept on it. I personally have done more *pro bono* work than is known, and a number of my partners and associates have done it, and at the other firms, the same is true. I don't know what the answer to it is. It's being explored now. I do think that the firms are going to have to take a good close look at it and make sure that they do whatever they can possibly do by way of performing that kind of work. I know that we've talked a little bit about it. I've talked with Frank Newton about it some. He happens to be one who believes strongly in that type of work being done. And I share his views completely. The big question is, how can you mechanically really get it done? I think that it's going to require probably two things; first, the realization that you cannot dictate to the large organization and say, well, we want so many men and women out of that firm to do *pro bono* work, because it's not going to work that way. And secondly, I think we're going to have to have some rethinking on the part of our larger firms—for them to cooperate and see what can be done to meet the need. I think once that is done, I think that the problem will be solved, at least in part. Now, let me say something to you about the Houston firms who believe in *pro bono.* I know these people; I'm with them often and I also know that they do a certain amount of *pro bono* work, but how effective has that been? How well it's been done is hard to tell because the individuals who have offered to do that work are not sufficiently specialized, sufficiently adept in some of the fields where it's most needed to do it. So, there's a problem immediately. But at least they've shown their readiness to want to do it and I think that they deserve credit for that.

Well, our time's up. I want to tell you that this has been a great experience for me, one of the most delightful ones that I have enjoyed. And I want to thank you for giving me the opportunity of being with you. Thank you very much.

Breinigsville, PA USA
06 November 2010
248768BV00001B/6/P